P9-DFN-332

THE TYPE B MANAGER

THE TYPE B MANAGER

*Leading Successfully
in a Type A World*

Victor Lipman

PRENTICE HALL PRESS

PRENTICE HALL PRESS
Published by the Penguin Group
Penguin Group (USA) LLC
375 Hudson Street, New York, New York 10014

USA • Canada • UK • Ireland • Australia • New Zealand • India • South Africa • China

penguin.com

A Penguin Random House Company

THE TYPE B MANAGER

Copyright © 2015 by Victor Lipman
Penguin supports copyright. Copyright fuels creativity, encourages diverse voices,
promotes free speech, and creates a vibrant culture. Thank you for buying an authorized
edition of this book and for complying with copyright laws by not reproducing, scanning,
or distributing any part of it in any form without permission. You are supporting writers
and allowing Penguin to continue to publish books for every reader.
PRENTICE HALL PRESS is a registered trademark of Penguin Group (USA) LLC.

ISBN: 978-0-7352-0543-7

This book has been registered with the Library of Congress.

First edition: August 2015

PRINTED IN THE UNITED STATES OF AMERICA

10 9 8 7 6 5 4 3 2 1

Text design by Laura K. Corless

Portions of some of these chapters appeared in Victor Lipman's blogs about management
for *Forbes* and *Psychology Today*. The section in Chapter 7 from *Sacred Hoops: Spiritual Lessons
of a Hardwood Warrior* by Phil Jackson with Hugh Delehanty, copyright © 1995 by Phil Jackson,
is used by permission of Hachette Books. The excerpt(s) from *Type A Behavior and Your Heart*
by Meyer Friedman and Ray H. Rosenman, copyright © 1974 by Meyer Friedman, are
used by permission of Alfred A. Knopf, an imprint of the Knopf Doubleday Publishing
Group, a division of Random House LLC. All rights reserved.

Names have been changed throughout the book, but situations have not.

While the author has made every effort to provide accurate telephone numbers, Internet
addresses, and other contact information at the time of publication, neither the publisher
nor the author assumes any responsibility for errors, or for changes that occur after
publication. Further, the publisher does not have any control over and does not
assume any responsibility for author or third-party websites or their content.

Most Prentice Hall Press books are available at special quantity discounts for bulk purchases for
sales promotions, premiums, fund-raising, or educational use. Special books, or book excerpts, can
also be created to fit specific needs. For details, write: Special.Markets@us.penguingroup.com.

658.4092
Lip

For Anna Lee, Alison and Bridget
My sun, moon and stars

Ingram

10/15

GERMANTOWN COMMUNITY LIBRARY
GERMANTOWN. WI 53022

CONTENTS

Part III
Putting It Together

INTRODUCTION

Whether you're a supervisor on the shop floor or an executive in the C-suite, you have an enormous amount of power over the employees who report to you. Think about it: You're often the person, other than perhaps a significant other or parent, who has the biggest impact on your employees' minute-to-minute, day-to-day, week-to-week, and month-to-month existence. If you're not working remotely (which only a small minority of the workforce is), your employees will probably see you often: in meetings, around the office or job site, at the watercooler or in the cafeteria, or simply whenever you're discussing whatever it is they're working on. You likely control their compensation and the way others in management perceive their job performance—in short, their livelihood.

A good relationship with a manager makes a bad job bearable, but a bad relationship with a manager can make a good job a misery.

So what makes a good manager? Are some personality types better suited for it than others? Given that management, at its core, involves accomplishing work through other people, the relationship between employee and manager is of central importance. People have to *want* to do work for others; even compensation and recognition have their limits. So what exactly are the personality traits that make others want to do their best for you? What are the qualities that make you successful as a manager?

It's a deceptively simple question because one thing we do know is that management isn't a simple job. Research has made it clear that there's currently an epidemic of employee disengagement. Numerous studies, as we'll see in more detail, indicate that between 60 and 70 percent of employees are "disengaged"—management code for not emotionally connected to their organizations and therefore in all likelihood not working at full productive capacity. If being a manager were easy, we'd never see such numbers.

As a young manager being considered for executive ranks at a Fortune 500 company many years ago, I had the same odd conversation, with only minor changes in phrasing, with several executives on different occasions. When discussing my future, the dialogue went like this:

Senior executive: "I just don't know about you. I can't quite put my finger on it, but you don't seem like a manager. You just don't seem like executive material."

To which I'd normally respond: "Why—what exactly is it that makes you say that?"

The answer would be: "I don't know . . . you seem too quiet, too soft-spoken, too calm—not authoritative enough."

By then I was managing complex projects like the company's annual report, working with a variety of people at all organizational levels—from CEOs and CFOs to product experts, accountants, designers, and printers. So I'd ask, "But doesn't it make more sense not to judge my personality, but to judge results? Do people generally like working for me? Do I get things done? Am I able to deliver large projects on time and on budget?"

And the concluding answer would be: "Yes, that's true, but I still just don't know. . . ."

Over time my own managers came to accept, for the most part, my personal style, my quietness, my soft-spokenness, my lack of excitability—in short, the absence of what are often called classic Type A personality characteristics. I ended up spending twenty-four years in management, becoming a vice president, and routinely overseeing advertising, marketing, and communications programs with annual budgets over $20 million. But the point here isn't about me. Like most people who spend decades in management I had successes and failures, strengths and weaknesses, good days and bad. I made so many mistakes over the years I used to say I could no longer remember the first couple hundred. It was only about a quarter century later that I began to think more about those earlier conversations, the puzzlement over my personal style, and what it meant about the common perceptions of managers and executives that we've so often come to expect.

Excellent managers come in all shapes and sizes. Like snowflakes, no two are exactly alike. Two of the most widely respected of the past half century, for example, have revealingly unique personalities. Phil Jackson, "Lord of the Rings" (a reference to the eleven NBA championship rings he's won as coach of the Chicago Bulls and the Los Angeles Lakers), is known for using an unorthodox blend of basketball wisdom, Zen Buddhism, and Lakota Sioux philosophy to bring his teams to peak performance. Warren Buffett, the "Oracle of Omaha," legendary investor with a net worth of over $60 billion, still lives in his first home, purchased for $31,500 in 1957. Though Jackson has been fortunate to coach some of the greatest basketball players in history (Michael Jordan, Scottie Pippen, Shaquille O'Neal, and Kobe Bryant), it was only when these supremely gifted individuals bought into Jackson's highly personal vision of team harmony that talent was translated into rings. Similarly, Buffett, who possesses one of the most incisive business minds ever, is known for his insistence on surrounding himself with the absolute best and brightest people he can and then backing off and giving them wide latitude to follow their own instincts. So much so that he's been called the "Delegator in Chief."

Neither of these enormously successful individuals conformed to any preconceived notions of how managers or coaches or executives should think or act. They both forged their own unique styles.

As a longtime manager, and one who's been fascinated for decades by both the challenges and satisfaction that management can bring, I have no desire to write a management textbook. But what I do want to do is explore from a manager's perspective, an insider's perspective, some of the key functions of management, the real pain points of management, and examine the personality traits that help you succeed as a manager—to better understand why some people are successful and others aren't. What you'll find, I believe, is that many of our most commonly held assumptions about what makes a successful manager are just plain wrong.

Consider the widely accepted stereotype of the hard-driving, demanding, highly stressed Type A executive. Most often this is what we just assume managers should be. But since management is all about accomplishing work through others, is this really the best sort of personality to make others *want* to do their best for you? Or might there be another style—a more relaxed, measured, lower-volume Type B approach, let's say, that can elicit at times even better results? We'll explore these questions in these pages.

Like a writer who needs to find his or her own voice or a baseball pitcher who needs to find the best arm angle for optimal delivery, all managers ultimately need to find their own personal styles. But even though there's no absolute right way to manage, there are broad themes that emerge when we examine successful management, best practices that often involve some skills and traits you might not normally associate with management success. Helping you uncover these qualities—and helping you become the best manager you can—is the purpose of this book.

PART I

The Big Picture

Research has shown that there's an epidemic of employee disengagement. Vast numbers of employees are not emotionally committed to their companies and not working at full productivity. These problems most often have their roots in manager-employee relationships. In order to find ways to boost employee engagement we first need to understand fully the importance of a manager and why personality plays so critical a role in management effectiveness.

CHAPTER 1

People Leave Managers, Not Companies

People say many things about managers:

> He's too demanding. She's too intense.
> He's a great motivator. Her team really likes working for her.
> You can count on him. She gets things done.
> He's a terrific leader. She's a real strategic thinker.
> He doesn't know what he's doing. She doesn't have a clue.

But there's one thing I'm willing to bet you never hear. You never hear people say management is an easy job.

After I retired from management in 2012, I wanted to step back and gain some perspective on what I'd been doing for the last quarter century. As I began to spend time with different organizations' management and employee studies, trying to get a broader sense of the common issues managers were grappling with and how they compared with my own experiences, one inescapable truth struck me: *Vast numbers of employees are disengaged.* By "disengaged," I mean not emotionally committed to the organizations they work for, and therefore in all likelihood not highly motivated and fully productive.

There are subtle differences in how different studies define "employee engagement," but the commonalities among the various studies are far more important than the differences. No matter how you slice the data, in the big picture somewhere around 60 or 70 percent of employees are simply not working—*say it straight*—as hard as they could be. Let's take some examples. Gallup data shows 30 percent of employees "engaged." Towers Watson data shows 35 percent "highly engaged." Dale Carnegie data shows 29 percent "fully engaged."[1] And these aren't small studies; the Gallup survey includes more than 350,000 respondents and the Towers Watson survey includes more than 32,000. Gallup goes on to estimate an annual cost in lost U.S. productivity of more than $450 billion. This is a staggering figure. Even if it's imprecise, it gives a sense of the magnitude of the problem.

What high-level factors contribute to this epidemic of disengagement? To return to the title of this chapter: "People leave managers, not companies." In short, the central relationship between manager and employee plays a critical role. Beyond that, other factors also contribute. These include belief in senior leadership, pride in one's company, and the chronic uncertainty resulting from a steady stream of reorganizations, layoffs, and pressure "to do more with less." But no matter the precise constellation of factors, which vary according to the character and circumstances of an organization, there's no question that a chronically high level of employee disengagement represents both a failure of management and a fundamental challenge to it: a challenge to do what is needed to keep vast numbers of individuals interested in their work, feeling good about their organizations, and working as productively as they can.

What does this high-level data mean to you as a manager? It means, first and hopefully encouragingly, that if you find the practice of management challenging, you're not alone. It *is* challenging and you have a great deal of company. If 60 to 70 percent of employees are working at less than full capacity, an awful lot of you in management are dealing with motivation problems. It also means there's a huge opportunity: an opportunity to better engage employees and improve productivity for your department and organization. To use simple numbers, if you manage ten employees and six of them are to some extent disengaged, and you can reach on average two of them to better engage and motivate them, those are immediately very significant productivity gains you'll achieve.

Of course the challenge lies in reaching those two employees, understanding why they feel the way they do, and improving their mindsets. We'll dissect these challenges and provide new tools to approach the old task of management in the pages ahead.

"Here's something they'll probably never teach you in business school," wrote Gallup CEO Jim Clifton in the summary accompanying his organization's 2013 "State of the American Workplace" employee engagement study. "The single biggest decision you make in your job—bigger than all the rest—is who you name manager. When you name the wrong person manager, nothing fixes that bad decision. Not compensation, not benefits—nothing."[2]

Management Insight

As a manager, you have an enormous amount of power. Most often you're the single most important influence on how motivated and productive your employees will be.

CHAPTER 2

The ABCs of Types A and B

How you view the world depends on the lens through which you see it: your background, your experiences, your education, your expectations. Adjust a lens slightly and vision changes as well.

As a manager, you may well spend time observing the behavior of other managers and their teams (I know I did), thinking about what works well and what doesn't, who commands respect and who doesn't, and why some individuals seem to have a natural gift for leadership while others are constantly wrestling with a dissatisfied, disgruntled staff. Management styles are as variable as personalities; no two are exactly alike. Yet when you step back, or rather move higher—say to the proverbial ten-thousand-foot vantage point—broad patterns emerge.

One day, I happened across information about studies conducted by Drs. Meyer Friedman and Ray Rosenman in the 1950s. In these pioneering studies, which were done to investigate the chances of certain types of individuals developing heart disease, Drs. Friedman and Rosenman clinically defined two broad personality types: Type A individuals and Type B individuals.

Type A personalities were characterized by qualities marked by a high degree of competitiveness, achievement orientation, and elevated stress levels—not what would generally be considered especially "people-focused" qualities. In the words of Drs. Friedman and Rosenman, "It is a particular complex of personality traits, including excessive competitive drive, aggressiveness, impatience, and harrying sense of time urgency."[1] In contrast, Type B personalities were more relaxed, reflective, quieter, slower to anger, and possessed lower stress levels. The researchers found that the more stressed, more tightly wound Type A individuals had a greater propensity for developing cardiac issues. It was groundbreaking work, forever adjusting the lens through which heart-related problems were viewed. The findings were described in Friedman and Rosenman's 1974 bestselling book, *Type A Behavior and Your Heart*. The notion of the Type A personality thus entered our national vocabulary and over the years became widely understood—even apart from any cardiac implications—as the personality type of a hard-driving high achiever, often perhaps extremely intelligent and capable but also with "workaholic" tendencies.

What intrigued me as I read about this research, most of which was done more than half a century ago, was something that had *not* been done with it. The implications of the findings had never in any meaningful way been applied to business.

Or, more specifically, to management.

Now think back on the managers you know. Chances are a large percentage of them, especially in the higher rungs of an organization, have Type A characteristics. They work hard, they play hard, they have great intensity and drive. With all the responsibilities, deadlines, and wrenching decisions to be regularly made, management is generally not the province of the laid-back. Though a study assessing the number of Type A's versus Type B's in management has never been done, after four decades in the workforce I have no doubt Type A's predominate. The only uncertainty is by how much.

Consider one other fundamental aspect of management. At its core, of course, management involves *accomplishing work through others*—and having others want to continue to do that work for you on an ongoing basis. The problem, if we accept the assumption that management has a high concentration of Type A personalities, is that some of their salient qualities—impatience, competitiveness, high stress levels—are not qualities that are easy to be on the receiving end of. Indeed, even many of the positive characteristics commonly associated with effective management—being authoritative, forceful, decisive—admirable qualities that help people make difficult decisions quickly and successfully deliver large, complex projects in a timely manner—are also qualities that have the potential to alienate. Let me state this clearly: Some Type A managers are unquestionably among the finest individuals I've ever had the privilege to know: brilliant, boundless energy, superior role models. But in the aggregate, the difficulties associated with Type A personalities take a managerial toll. It's just human nature—most people chafe under too much authority, too much forcefulness, too much control.

"Now, there's one phrase I hate to see on any executive's evaluation, no matter how talented he may be, and that's the line: 'He has trouble getting along with other people,'" wrote Lee Iacocca, former Chrysler chairman and CEO, in *Iacocca: An Autobiography* (with William Novak). "To me, that's the kiss of death. 'You've just destroyed the guy,' I always think. 'He can't get along with people? Then he's got a real problem, because that's all we've got around here. No dogs, no apes—only people. And if he can't get along with his peers, what good is he to the company? As an executive, his whole function is to motivate other people. If he can't do that, he's in the wrong place.'"

These lines were written in 1984, and the only addition I'd suggest today would be to include "or she" in the first sentence about the hypothetical executive. But the point about the fundamental importance of "getting along with other people" couldn't be said better. Because that's who you as a manager have to be at your best with. *No dogs, no apes—only people.*

Given this perspective on the macro-level managerial environment, is it surprising we have chronic employee disengagement levels hovering around 60 to 70 percent? I don't believe it's surprising at all. But what options do we have? Well, let's consider the core qualities of the Type B individual: the calmness, the slowness to anger, the patience and thoughtfulness in dealing with others. These are all qualities that people find easy to work with.

Is it reasonable to expect that high-performing organizations will ever be completely dominated by the more easygoing and people-oriented style of the Type B manager? Such managers possess numerous qualities—they're good listeners, open communicators, of calm demeanor—that help them build the all-important closer rapport with their employees. But will they be consistently able to make the hard decisions and drive productivity with the urgency business requires? Perhaps not always so easily.

But there are clear benefits that a more measured Type B approach confers. And there is also a constructive middle ground where Type A's can gain some helpful Type B characteristics to build more "engaged" employee relationships and where Type B's can elevate their intensity to drive just a bit harder for the results business requires. While a leopard may not be able to change its spots, as the saying goes, it's certainly possible to make changes at the managerial margins. Add some more B to the A, add more A to the B—this balance can be a constructive intersection. Personalities of course are endlessly individual and variable. But whatever the ultimate makeup, a solid dose of Type B characteristics is a valuable element in the managerial mix.

There are numerous different psychological frameworks by which to categorize personalities. From Sigmund Freud to Carl Jung to Abraham Maslow (who focused on a hierarchy of needs) to David McClelland (who focused on key elements of motivation) to the Myers-Briggs Type Indicator (currently used extensively in business), among others, there are well-conceived paradigms that help explain and order human behavior. But the Type A / Type B framework, long neglected, has particular relevance for management. It's simple, practical, and has great potential, as Type A managers are so prevalent and Type B qualities so potentially useful.

Is the Type A / Type B framework a perfect lens through which to view management? There's little perfection in life and certainly not in something so messily complex as management. But it *is* a unique and helpful lens through which to view the management experience. It readily helps you isolate problems that occur. *More importantly, it leads you to practical solutions to improve management performance.*

"When D + D + D = A"

Since little has been written about how Type A and B personalities can be applied to management, it was with considerable
interest that I noticed a blog in the *Harvard Business Review*,
titled "How Type-A People Can Play Nice with Others," while
I was completing this manuscript in the summer of 2014.

Written by Melissa Raffoni, a CEO/management consultant,
the article, as the title suggests, directly acknowledges the
challenges that high-octane Type A behavior can pose. "People
have always commented on the fact that I am highly driven,"
Raffoni wrote, "a 'Type A' to a T. I set personal goals, manage
multiple projects at once, and run at the speed of light."

She offers a blunt self-assessment of the effects of this
behavior. "I've discerned three behavioral tendencies of
Type-A performers, which I refer to as the High D curse. They
are a tendency to *dominate*, to be *demanding*, and to be (or
appear to be) *distracted*. While embracing the blessings of
being Type-A, being aware of my own demon traits helps me
keep them in check." Why does Raffoni feel this is needed?
"What comes with this high-performing personality," she
writes, "is the tendency to—let's just say it—piss people off or
push them away."

Multiply this tendency by the vast number of Type A's in
management and we begin to understand why employee
engagement numbers are chronically low. Raffoni offers three
suggestions for Type A's: (1) to stop dominating others,
create—and stick to—a plan; (2) to be less demanding, focus
on empathy; and (3) to avoid getting distracted, minimize
interruptions.

Her conclusion? "All this said, I'm so grateful for the Type
A's in the world—but all of us in this club need to strive to be

more self-aware and mindful. Whether at home or at work, we need to adjust if we want to have richer relationships and be better managers."

I respect her insights. And admire her candor.

Management Insight

Since management is all about accomplishing work through others, the personality of the manager, and how he or she relates to employees, has a major impact on employee engagement and motivation. The core qualities of the Type B manager—including calmness, thoughtfulness, and patience—are qualities that people find easy to work with.

PART II

Managing for Productivity

This section describes, from a grassroots management perspective, key managerial functions and behaviors that can make a difference in your employees' level of engagement and productivity. These include motivation, objective setting, handling conflict, employee development, conducting effective evaluations, dealing with difficult employees, and many others. The strengths and weaknesses of Type A and Type B managers in various situations are explored. While Type A characteristics involving control and authority are usually viewed as the backbone of traditional management, Type B qualities involving lower stress and stronger personal connections often make the difference between employee commitment and indifference, motivation and demotivation, success and failure.

CHAPTER 3

Motivating and Demotivating

The Power of Beer

One of the central challenges for managers is that it's not especially easy to motivate employees, but it's all too easy to demotivate them. There are aspects of the Type A managerial personality that can inadvertently demotivate an employee. At times, for example, a manager's fundamental intensity or force of personality can send a message that is actually quite different from what is intended. Simply put, what is sent is not always what is received, and such misunderstandings can have unexpected consequences. Let's consider an example.

Donna was the owner of a small business that made changes to improve the quality of its website, upgrading and enhancing the visual impact of numerous product offerings displayed on the site. Donna was proud of the changes; she had closely overseen the project and spent considerable time with it. A week after the upgraded site launched, Donna was speaking casually about a variety of business matters with one of her employees, Nancy, her accountant. At one point the conversation turned to the website, and, without thinking anything of it, Nancy mentioned that no, she hadn't yet taken a look at the revised site.

Donna, a forthright, intense person who had a tendency to verbalize whatever was passing through her mind at that moment, exclaimed, *"That's pathetic!"* Nancy was immediately taken aback.

What Donna actually meant to communicate was "We've put a lot of work into the new site and are proud of it, and I'm just surprised that as an employee of this company you haven't taken the time to look at it yet." But despite this benign intent, the two words that actually came out of her mouth had a far different effect. They disturbed Nancy, who was stung by them, and she turned them over in her mind for several weeks.

"She thinks I'm pathetic," Nancy thought to herself. "All because I didn't look quickly enough at her new website. Is this really the kind of person I want to work for?"

From a manager's standpoint, it can be frustratingly easy to demotivate your employees. Coming from a hard-driving, demanding Type A business owner, Donna's two-word exclamation was nothing more than a momentary expression of frustration that was forgotten nearly as soon as she'd spoken it. Donna in fact had a very high opinion of Nancy, whom she considered a valuable, capable employee. She had no idea her words had bothered Nancy and would have been shocked to learn that Nancy continued to nurse lingering hurt feelings about the brief exchange for weeks afterward.

Let's take a look at some ways managers can easily demotivate employees, often hardly being aware they're doing so. This is by no means an exhaustive list (that's one of the real challenges of management—there are many easy ways to go awry):

Using your stature in a way that indicates you don't fully respect your employees as individuals. These can be subtle oversights in day-to-day operations that add up over time. Being chronically late for meetings with your employees. Not returning their messages. Ignoring suggestions for improving grassroots operations. These may seem like trivial things to an executive with weightier strategic issues on his or her mind, but the reality is people care about them and resent when they are ignored. Over time they can constitute an irksome pattern of almost unconscious behavior, barely noticed by a manager but highly visible to an employee who is, for instance, frequently kept waiting by someone whose time appears to be more important than the employee's own. (We'll cover this issue in greater detail in Chapter 11, "Small Things Make a Big Difference.")

Not providing enough recognition. Employee recognition is a little like ice cream: An awful lot of people just can't seem to get enough of it. In nearly a quarter century of management, lack of recognition was the *one* issue that surfaced repeatedly on literally every employee survey I was personally involved with. We'll assume of course it's deserved (as giving undeserved recognition does nothing but erode a manager's credibility). Whether that recognition is formal or informal—from an official award to a quiet pat on the back—there's always a strong appetite for it that managers will never go wrong bearing in mind.

There are management schools of thought that compensation is not motivating, and employees are motivated only by other aspects of their work environment, but the simplest and best answer I've seen to this question comes from longtime GE CEO Jack Welch in his book (coauthored with Suzy Welch), *Winning*. "I'll never forget the time I was at a meeting about how GE should reward the winner of the Steinmetz Award, given annually to the company's best scientist. I was a group VP at the time, and so my ears really perked up when one of the vice chairmen, a guy with a lot of stature and a lot of dough, registered his opinion. 'These people don't want money,' he said, 'they want recognition.'

"He must have forgotten where he came from!

"Of course, people want to be recognized for great performance. Plaques and public fanfare have their place. But without money, they lose a lot of their impact. Even the Nobel and Pulitzer prizes come with cash awards."

Losing your temper. This is an easy one. Again, it's just human nature: People dislike being on the wrong end of this sort of thing. Lost tempers are often followed by lost loyalty. Some employees are thick-skinned and can take it. For others, like our accountant Nancy, merely being the object of a poorly chosen phrase, not even close to a full loss of temper, can lead to a week or more of glum introspection.

Being chronically distant. This is the informal cousin of "not providing enough recognition" noted earlier. Employees don't respond well to managers who are distant. They like at least some level of emotional connection. They may not need constant affirmation, but they do want to know they're doing a good job and are valued. Simple words of occasional encouragement are easy and have a common cost: nothing.

Let's look at some easy ways management can motivate. Keep in mind we're not focusing on compensation in this discussion, which is sometimes beyond the control of individual managers. Compensation of course—such as large incentive compensation programs—can be highly motivating, especially to executives where bonus payouts are a key element of their compensation structure. But for these purposes, I'm not focusing on compensation and benefits, but on day-to-day managerial tactics that *are* within any manager's power to control.

Support employee growth in numerous forms. Employees perform best when their environment is conducive to growth. That growth can take many forms: career growth, professional growth (the opportunity to acquire new skills), personal growth (an atmosphere supportive of friendships and networking), and, naturally, financial growth. Many studies support the importance of employees making progress on a daily basis, having the opportunity to advance their careers and work in a friendly setting. The opportunity to grow makes a positive difference, just as the absence of growth opportunities has an immediate chilling effect. Good managers recognize the near-universal appeal of growth and take time to foster it.

Take a genuine interest in your employees' work-life balance. To the extent that managers can offer flexibility in schedules, and are understanding about family commitments—doctors' and dentists' appointments and so forth—their employees will greatly appreciate the consideration. What happens outside work almost always influences how an employee performs within it. Even small gestures can make a big difference.

Listen. This is an easy one: Just listen thoughtfully. To employees' ideas for job improvements, or their problems, concerns, frustrations, conflicts, dramas, kids' issues, parents' issues, grandparents' issues . . . you name it, I've heard it. You have to separate the wheat from the chaff, and as a manager it can wear you out at times, but within reason, intelligent listening is an integral part of the job. If someone is a chronic malingerer and talks for the sake of talking, just let that person know it's time to get back to work. But if someone is a good employee . . . well, people appreciate being heard.

Do unto others as you would have done unto you. When it comes to treatment of subordinates, this is about as universal as it gets. But it's powerful too, and just as valid today as it was a few thousand years ago.

Even if you're a thoughtful and perceptive Type B manager, one thing you'll never go wrong with is occasionally thinking outside the norms to motivate creatively. Here you're limited only by your imagination, though I will add that in four decades in the workforce, there was only one motivator I personally came across that caused large numbers of individuals to immediately improve their job performance.

Back then I was a young man loading trucks for a large national trucking company. The problem management faced was "missorts," too many packages chronically loaded onto the wrong trucks, resulting in costly delivery delays. The section of the plant I worked in had six trucks, all bound for different parts of the United States, backed up to bays in front of which boxes flowed by on a conveyor belt. Two people worked each truck: a "pickoff person" who picked the boxes off the conveyor belt, and a loader who stacked the boxes inside the truck. It was a fast operation and boxes moved quickly. Try as one might to read all labels carefully, in the sea of boxes up to fifty pounds flowing down the belt, a pickoff person generally misread a few labels during each shift.

This problem could be virtually eliminated if the loader also read the labels inside the truck, thus providing a double check. The unfortunate reality, however, was that we loaders strongly disliked double-checking the labels. The trucks had little light in them, so it was difficult to see, and it was bitter cold in winter and sweltering in summer. Loading was OK when one was left alone to a continuous rhythm of hard, mindless labor, but straining to read each label in dim light added a markedly stressful element. For the most part management accepted the situation, occasionally pushing for more diligent inside-the-truck double-checking, but generally acknowledging the task's inherent difficulty.

At one point, however, when missorts became too costly a problem, a creative member of the management team devised a new incentive program. Overnight it changed all of the loaders' collective behavior and resolved the problem.

The motivator was disarmingly simple: Molson beer.

If a two-person loading team achieved no missorts for an entire week, we were each rewarded at the end of work on Friday night of the following week with a case of Molson's. Suddenly the highly motivated loaders worked with new diligence, fervor, and visual

"Putting the 'Cent' in Incentives"

Want to have a better chance to motivate employees at all levels of your organization? Design financial incentives so employees at all levels can benefit from them. There's a natural tendency for management to focus most heavily on senior-level financial incentives (aka bonuses). While this is understandable, it's best not to neglect substantive incentives for lower-level employees—that is, if you expect them to be vigorously committed to an enterprise's success. But will so broad an incentive program be unduly costly? Naturally the plan has to be carefully structured so additional payouts reflect clearly defined revenue and/or earnings targets.

acuity. I remember those days fondly. Life was good. I was twenty-three and had cases of beer stacked literally up to the ceiling of my small apartment.

The point of course is not that beer is a motivational panacea (though some might argue otherwise), but that carefully chosen creative motivators can have a surprisingly positive effect. In this instance, our manager, a young, soft-spoken, affable Type B sort of fellow, had, without once raising his voice, completely changed the problematic behavior of a challenging group: a pretty rowdy bunch of truck loaders. He'd come up with an incentive that was perfect for its target, male blue-collar workers in their twenties.

Management Insight

It can be easy for Type A managers to demotivate simply by the force of their personality, even when they have absolutely no intention of doing so. Type B's often have natural advantages when it comes to motivating employees by their relaxed, inviting way of taking the time to get to know them as individuals and gaining insights into what they value.

CHAPTER 4

Management Without High Standards Isn't Management At All

The management approach I'm advocating in these pages isn't a "touchy-feely" exercise in management sensitivity training. Just as Type A managers are prone to certain weaknesses, they have undeniable strengths; and just as Type B managers have undeniable strengths, they are prone to certain weaknesses.

One clear challenge for the likable, more people-oriented Type B manager is the tendency not to drive for the sort of above-and-beyond results that management, and indeed the realities of competitive business, often require. In this regard, the experience of Dave, a promising young manager, is instructive.

Dave was a highly regarded young executive at a large financial services company. He was bright and had an MBA and a keen marketing mind. His team liked him and his colleagues liked him. He had an open, approachable style—relaxed and even-tempered. Unlike many managers in the conservative organization, who were felt often to be demanding without being good communicators, Dave was an anomaly. He was unusually sensitive to the needs of his employees and supportive of them. In return they rewarded him with loyalty.

While this may sound like an excellent working arrangement—and in fact it was comfortable and harmonious—there was one substantive problem: Dave's teams were not delivering large product rollouts as quickly and effectively as they were expected to. Being highly attuned to the needs of his employees, when they needed time off for personal matters, Dave gave it to them. And when they complained that individuals in other departments were being difficult to work with and slowing things down, he was sympathetic to his team's concerns. But he never really "got his hands dirty" wading into the conflicts to resolve them.

When deadlines began to slip, Dave argued on his team's behalf, explaining to his own management the difficulty of the assignment and the frustrating circumstances his team was battling. When other colleagues in management team meetings were occasionally critical of the pace at which Dave's team seemed to be progressing, he fully supported his team members. New product rollouts were always complex, multifaceted projects, he'd point out, and his people were working with tight resources in a tight time frame. And when the project was delivered several weeks past deadline, he defended his team against criticisms from other managers.

This pattern repeated itself on several projects. His team was outstanding, Dave would say, but because of the task's inherent difficulty they just couldn't deliver it on time. But his people were talented, he maintained, and always giving their best. In baseball parlance Dave was a classic "player's manager." He supported his players, but his team just couldn't produce the results the "front office" needed. Dave's own management soon grew weary of this recurring cycle. They recognized that Dave had some excellent managerial qualities—he was a bright young executive with good marketing instincts and fine "people skills"—but in the end they felt they had no alternative. Dave couldn't deliver the results his own management needed, so they let him go.

One thing I've always respected about management is that it's an exceptionally results-oriented enterprise. A good manager has to deliver strong results or he or she isn't really a good manager. Type B managers in particular need to keep this fundamental truth in mind. It's great to have happy employees. But if happy employees aren't sufficiently productive, a key piece is missing in the managerial puzzle.

Regardless of whether managers are Type A or Type B personalities—more controlling or more easygoing—a critical question is always: What level of standards are they managing to? Are they expecting and receiving excellence? How are they determining the goals and objectives their teams will be accountable for? If the bar is consistently set too high, it's a recipe for frustration. But if the bar is consistently set too low, it's a recipe for failure.

A tendency to avoid conflict and confrontation is a challenge many Type B managers face, and we'll deal with that in detail in Chapter 16 and elsewhere. For now, it's important to understand that in Dave's case, his team was emotionally committed but not highly productive. He'd developed a close emotional bond with his team members, but that closeness also made him unwilling to push them as hard as needed, or to address conflicts when he should have. He functioned more as a friend than as a manager with legitimate authority.

Dave excelled at something, but it wasn't quite management.

Management Insight

Respect, not friendship, is what a manager needs. Expect excellence. All managers, but Type B managers in particular, need to be sure they're holding their teams fully accountable, managing for productivity and driving for optimal results.

CHAPTER 5

"Bring Me My Shoes"

Communicating Without Alienating

I was a new employee, not yet a manager myself, just starting to learn the ways of the business world. Cathy, another new employee, a bright young lady who was becoming a good friend, was sitting in the cubicle next to mine. It was early on a Monday morning and the corporate air had the pleasant productive smell of hot coffee. Then Cathy's phone rang. Taylor, Cathy's manager, was calling from another wing of our sprawling headquarters.

I couldn't hear all of the conversation but I could hear enough. I heard Taylor barking, "Bring me my shoes!" and sounding rather ferocious. She was speaking so loudly Cathy was holding the phone a bit away from her ear. Evidently Taylor, who kept a formidable shoe collection in the closet in her office, was in another part of the compound and needed a new pair of shoes—fast!—for a major Monday morning meeting.

Cathy was flustered. She was new to the job, and both the physical layout of the headquarters and the details of the shoe collection were large and confusing. I could hear more random growling over the phone about the specifics of the shoe request, and then Cathy hung up. I felt bad I couldn't help her, but I too was new and could hardly find my own way around, barely able to locate my car at day's end in our massive parking lot. Shaking her head, a forlorn-looking Cathy hurriedly left to search for the right shoes.

Predictably, the working relationship between Cathy and Taylor didn't last long. Within a few months Cathy left the company, tired of being barked at and asked to perform outlandish tricks well outside the scope of any reasonable job description.

I never knew a good manager who wasn't a good communicator. Like integrity it's a foundational management quality. Lacking it, you'll always be a trout swimming upstream—meaning managing others will always be a struggle.

Many Type B's are by nature open communicators, and this attribute serves them well in a management role. So much of productive management is dependent on meaningful, effective communication. It determines how assignments are made, how feedback is given, and how rewards and punishments are administered. It's the daily fabric of manager-employee life, and it's a core management skill at which Type B's excel. Type A's are more uneven in this regard. While some are truly exceptional (indeed, they can spellbind an audience of thousands with their public communication skills in addition to being highly articulate in "one on ones"), others may have little time or patience for this skill. As we saw in Chapter 3 on motivating and demotivating, with Donna, the small business owner, an intense, shoot-first-and-ask-questions-later communication style easily leads to unwanted, unintended consequences.

But an even more pervasive, problematic management communication issue was once pointed out to me by a Human Resources colleague.

We were attending an in-house management seminar on employee engagement. At the time the company we both worked for had lower employee engagement scores than it would have liked, and the scores were trending in a negative direction. During a break, the HR executive and I were discussing some of the challenges of management. "Well, you don't have to worry too much," she said to me. "You're a good manager." Her comment surprised me. Actually, I felt management was difficult. At that stage of my career I was still learning to deal more directly with conflict and employees' performance-related issues, and didn't feel at all competent at it. "Why do you say that?" I asked—not fishing for a compliment so much as curious to understand what she considered the elements of good management. To this day, decades later, I still remember her five-word answer.

"You talk to your people," she said.

When I asked her what exactly she meant by that, she added, "I've seen how you relate to them—you communicate with them, you have some idea what's going on with them."

"You mean a lot of managers don't?" I asked.

"You'd be surprised," she said.

Years later I now have more context for that conversation, and more appreciation of it. Open, honest communication of course is the foundation for all good relationships—be it a friendship, a marriage, or the relationship between manager and employee. Ideally, managers need to take the time to get to know their employees—a need that has become increasingly challenging with remote management situations.

Employees respond best when they're treated in a predictable not capricious manner. They then know what to expect. I never at all minded working for a tough, demanding manager so long as I felt the manager was fair and consistent. Problems arise when a manager's actions fluctuate wildly—encouraging and supportive one day but distant and irritable the next. On the other side of the consistency coin, I can't put it simpler than this: Erratic management behavior alienates. It makes people nervous. Employees don't want to deal with it. They want a steady manager they can count on. How often are employees disturbed by bosses who run unaccountably hot and cold? Inconsistent managerial behavior leaves employees uncertain, disengaged, afraid of losing their jobs, and prone to act defensively. And if people are spending much of their time acting defensively, it's a safe bet they won't be doing their best work.

Ultimately, when it comes to communication, it matters less whether a manager is loud or soft-spoken, forceful or reserved, Type A or Type B, so long as the manager is credible, trustworthy, and treats an employee with respect.

Returning now to our unfortunate Shoe Mission that opened this chapter, it was also only much later that I began to think more about the broader implications of that morning. This was impulsive Type A management at its most needlessly destructive. It also brings up broader questions regarding the treatment of subordinates, in terms of the normal pattern of interactions between manager and employee.

How is communication routinely handled and authority exercised? Is a manager autocratic and bullying, or considerate and patient? Erratic and impulsive, or consistent and fair? Does a relationship motivate or demoralize?

No less formidable a figure of authority than General Douglas MacArthur, a highly respected U.S. general in the Pacific theater in World War II, has provided perspective on some of these matters.* Among his "Principles of Leadership," seventeen bulleted points (shown in their entirety in the Appendix), are two basic questions that even today remind me of the Shoe Mission:

- Do I heckle my subordinates or strengthen and encourage them?
- Do I act in such a way as to make my subordinates *want* to follow me?

One thing I know for certain is how Cathy would have answered those questions about her own management. Unfortunately, she didn't stay around long enough for anyone to get the chance to ask her.

....

*General MacArthur, hardly known for being a meek soul himself, was ultimately relieved of his command in Korea in 1951 by President Truman over the general's desire to expand the Korean conflict by attacking China. It was arguably the most serious military-civilian confrontation in U.S. history.

"The Dying Art of In-Person Communication"

Honesty questions of the day: How often do you send an email or text to someone to avoid in-person communication? How often do you call someone after hours or before hours so you can leave a message and avoid a real live conversation? I know I did these things when I was in business. Though hopefully not too often. With the multitude of ever-growing social media technologies at our disposal, there's a danger that good old-fashioned in-person talking to someone may become a lost art. That would be very bad news. Following are clear business benefits of direct as opposed to indirect communication:

> **It's a dialogue, not a monologue**—A true exchange of thoughts, not a verbal one-way street.

> **It offers the opportunity for nuanced messages**—Far beyond the constraints of a three-minute voicemail or even the lengthiest of texts.

> **Problems can be openly discussed and resolved**—This of course may involve conflict (and, worse still, unpleasantness!), but it's also the way meaningful collaborative solutions are reached.

When I was a manager, I literally found it physically hard to sit still in one place for a long time. This often led to my using the well-documented practice of "management by walking around," a therapeutic way of relieving for me some of the tedium of bureaucracy. As a consequence of wandering, I found myself talking to my employees. I got to know them better because of it. I got to hear about their families, their kids' sports, their aging parents, their dentist appointments, their cats, their dogs, their hopes and dreams and frustrations on the job and off.

It was good, it was helpful. I may have wasted some of their time—no doubt I did—but it gave me added context to understand how well, or not, my employees were doing their jobs. It can do the same for you.

Management Insight

Open communication is a fundamental skill at which Type B managers excel. Communication that is impulsive and capricious can easily demotivate, while communication that is consistent and thoughtful fosters employee trust.

CHAPTER 6

All Good Managers Lead by Example

While it's hard to disagree in theory with the idea that leading by example is a management best practice, business headlines are regularly populated by managers who do not. Today's media coverage of business sometimes reads like an encyclopedia of management malfeasance—involving insider trading, theft, embezzlement, money laundering, accounting irregularities, securities fraud, plain old abuse of power, and on and on.

Personally, I was never a big fan of Robert McNamara, often described as the "architect of the Vietnam War" as U.S. secretary of defense in the 1960s, and later the head of the World Bank. But when it comes to the importance of leading by example, I never heard a better, more concise description than one from McNamara, back in the days when he was a young executive at Ford. Wrote Chrysler CEO Lee Iacocca in *Iacocca: An Autobiography*: "McNamara used to say that the boss had to be more Catholic than the Pope—and as clean as a hound's tooth."*

I'm not sure a hound's tooth is really all that clean (at least not the teeth of my hounds), but I do understand McNamara's intended meaning: When it comes to their actions, managers should be absolutely beyond a shadow of reproach.

"More Catholic than the Pope"—setting this kind of managerial example is an admirable behavioral goal. In fact, business ethics wasn't often taught back when I was in business school several decades ago. I'm glad it's a core component of many MBA programs today. Of course ethical behavior isn't something that's readily learned from a book; it's more part of one's emotional and psychological DNA. Ethical shortcomings aren't restricted to a certain personality type. They span the spectrum—though perhaps to the extent that Type A's are more driven, some of them may also be more easily led astray by the myriad temptations of the richly compensated business world. It's also reasonable to assume that certain Type B characteristics—such as being slower to anger, more patient and empathetic—are qualities that can help guide one toward "doing

....

*In his autobiography, Iacocca noted that McNamara did in fact practice what he preached. "He wasn't always easy to get along with, and his high standards of personal integrity could sometimes drive you crazy. Once, for a skiing vacation he planned, he needed a car with a ski rack. 'No problem,' I told him, 'I'll put a rack on one of our company cars out in Denver, and you just pick it up.' But he wouldn't hear of it. He insisted that we rent him a car from Hertz, pay extra for the ski rack and send him the bill. He resolutely refused to use a company car on his vacation, even though we loaned out hundreds of courtesy cars every weekend to other VIPs."

the right thing" when ethical dilemmas arise. Taking your time, not rushing to judgment, remaining rational, logical, and grounded in the face of a serious moral decision—all of these are part of a more deliberate mindset that can lead management to constructive, not hasty, resolutions.

But even beyond the somewhat nebulous world of ethics, there are highly practical reasons why leading by example—exhibiting consistently sound ethical behavior—makes excellent business sense.

It's effective.
It gets results.
It makes people want to follow you.

It sets the right tone for those in the lower levels of an organization, who—make no mistake about it—are always carefully watching how their leaders behave. It disarms any resentment that may be felt, rightly or wrongly, toward those in high managerial places. It's difficult to resent managers who roll up their sleeves and wade into the trenches when they need to, who share the same hardships their teams do. As famed philosopher and physician Albert Schweitzer once put it, "Example is not the main thing in influencing others; it is the only thing."

On the flip side of this behavioral coin, however—being an uneven role model, behaving badly, abusing power, not adhering to the same standards you ask others to adhere to—is the surest and most needless way to undermine your own management authority. We've all seen the headlines—the Enrons, the Madoffs, the systemic greed that almost brought down our global economy in 2008—the spectacular demolitions, the fiery crashes and burns. But far more commonplace and ultimately more destructive are the smaller, subtler, everyday problems—the questionable decisions that quietly erode faith in management and keep employee engagement numbers down around those abysmally low levels. Here's one such episode.

Over the years I went through so many reorganizations I can no longer remember them all, or even the details associated with most of them. But there's one I do recall clearly, though for the wrong reasons. As usual, the company was working with an external staff-reduction consultant, and it was a lengthy process in which each level of management was analyzed separately, one at a time, starting at the top, with such analyses "cascading" all the way down the organization until ultimately reaching the nonmanagement employee level.

The analysis thus started at the C-suite level—with all of the company's employees naturally watching closely to gain insight as to how deep the cuts would be, since lower levels would soon be affected. There were roughly ten executives at the C-suite level, and it was common knowledge throughout the company that one of the lines of business was doing poorly and likely would soon be closed down. But when the analysis was concluded and it came to the C-suite reductions, it turned out no one was cut. The failing line of business was in fact closed down, but a new position was created for the head of that business.

Initially, the rank-and-file employees didn't know quite what to make of the situation. Perhaps, they thought optimistically, the reductions would be fairly light after all. But as the layoff process—the subsequent analysis of each management level—cascaded down,

"You're Paying Me for My Opinion"

As anyone who's been around large, or even not so large, organizations knows, there's a subtle but common tendency to say what you think others in positions of power want to hear, regardless of the accuracy of the information. Not surprisingly, at times individuals can perceive economic benefits from behaving in this fashion. I'll say this as delicately as I can: This isn't a good thing. Altering reality to gain favor with those in power is never a good thing.

It's not good for the individual, who's subverting his or her actual experience, thoughts, and opinions. It's not good for the individual's manager, who is losing the benefit of genuine data and input. It's not good for the organization that is losing the benefit of a diversity of perspectives in solving challenging problems.

Early in my career I worked for an executive—as intense a Type A personality as I ever reported to—who made a point of telling his superiors: *"You're paying me for my opinion. If you're not paying me for my opinion—if you're paying me to tell you just what you want to hear—then you're paying me too much."*

I always felt it was one of the wisest things I ever heard in business.

When confronted with a difficult business decision, don't just say what you think your boss wants to hear. Don't just say what you think your CEO wants to hear. Don't just say what you think your board of directors wants to hear. Say what you, after thoughtful, measured Type B analysis and deliberation, believe to be right and best for your organization. Be your own man, be your own woman. An additional but not inconsequential side benefit: You'll sleep better at night knowing you're being true to your own personal values.

it soon became clear that reductions would be substantial—generally in the 20 to 30 percent range and sometimes higher.

The unsurprising result? Employee morale plummeted. Even if many at the company grudgingly accepted that substantive cost reductions were necessary, the real pain point, the lasting sand-in-the-sore issue, was that the leaders at the organization's highest level hadn't shared in the sacrifices they were asking others to make.

Nothing erodes employee morale more completely than watching management not play by the same rules they ask others to play by, not adhere to the same standards they expect others will. Nothing undermines a manager's position more profoundly.

The real tragedy is that these types of problems are preventable. They have absolutely nothing to do with ability, but everything to do with character, judgment, and self-discipline. Robert McNamara had it right. A manager should be "more Catholic than the Pope." And not just because it's somehow "nice" or ethical, but because it sets the right managerial tone. It's an awful lot easier for people to follow someone they believe in than someone they don't.

Management Insight

It's not reasonable to expect employees to follow a manager they don't fully respect. The most compelling reason for a Type B manager to always lead by example? It's effective.

CHAPTER 7

Team Building

Find Me a Good Cat Herd

Jim, the head of a major mutual fund company, was speaking to a group of executives about the qualities that had most helped him in the business world. He was a big, burly, outspoken, plainspoken fellow, with an outstanding track record of success—highly respected throughout his own organization as well as the industry. He was summing up what he believed were his own key attributes.

"Truth is, I'm not really an investment expert," he said.

That got the crowd's attention, as he was after all heading an investment company.

"I'm not really a product expert," he continued.

"I'm not really a customer service expert."

"I'm not really a systems or operations guy."

He paused. The room was completely quiet.

"But I'll tell you what I am," he said softly. "More than anything, I'm a team builder."

He shifted his considerable weight, looking a little like an aging NFL defensive lineman. "Oh sure, I know something about investing and product design and service and operations and all that. I've been in this business awhile now. But many of you in this room know more about those things than I do. No doubt about it. But one thing I can do, I can get all kinds of people to work together—that's one thing I do understand."

Of the many skills useful for success as a manager, one of the oddest may also be one of the most valuable. It's not hard to find managers who are outstanding numbers crunchers, customer service experts, or even individuals with creativity and vision. But if I need to get a complex, costly, critical project done, let me first find a manager who can herd cats.

Cats, of course, unlike "herd animals" such as horses, sheep, or buffalo, prefer to go their own way. Much like humans in a corporation. Though organizations want and need, as the name implies, to *organize* people toward common goals, the reality is that most human beings have their own ideas, agendas, and preferences. Which is why, when you have a really big important project—like building a jet engine or a computer, say, or producing an annual report or a Super Bowl commercial, or changing a company's culture—with many team members who have diverse skill sets and personalities . . . well, finding a manager talented enough to herd cats is a great place to start.

Fact is, very little of value is accomplished in an organization without collaboration, without large numbers of people working together toward a common goal. Thus, companies have an inexhaustible need for managers who can get people to put aside differences and work together effectively (easier said than done). These extremely valuable individuals exhibit a high degree of what could be called—my own term—"teamplayerism." In essence, it's the ability to work effectively with all kinds of people, to not be sidetracked by the inevitable disputes that arise, and to keep everyone on a positive, constructive course. The basic inclination to "reach out, connect, and include" makes Type B managers good natural team builders.

In many ways our mutual fund company friend Jim was a classic Type B personality. Open, friendly, conversational, he could talk in his easygoing manner to anyone about anything. He was always on the lookout for potential and finding ways to bring out the best in others. I remember spending a few hours with him at the end of the day at the bar in a hospitality tent on the eighteenth hole of a golf tournament one of our companies was sponsoring. We'd been there awhile, all had a few beers, and had been chatting amiably with, among others, the bartender, a very bright, pleasant young woman in her early twenties named Ramona. We were all impressed by her. She was professional and perceptive—just a nice, attractive personality who could more than hold her own with a group of slightly inebriated financial services executives in their forties and fifties. As evening fell and we finally got up to leave, Jim took a long look back at her as she started to clean things up behind the bar.

I could see he was thinking about something.

"Hey, Ramona," he said at last with a bit of a beer-tinged laugh but also a touch of seriousness, "you wanna sell any mutual funds?"

Jim was always building his team, even in the unlikeliest of circumstances.

The most famous team builder, the most high-profile cat herder of our time, is arguably Phil Jackson. Jackson, who's won eleven NBA championships as coach of the Chicago Bulls and the Los Angeles Lakers, is known for using a unique blend of basketball wisdom, Zen Buddhism, and Lakota Sioux philosophy to help his teams reach peak performance. But his greatest accomplishment, the foundation on which all of his success is built, is getting supremely gifted individual performers to think of team first and individual achievements second. Here's how he explains it in his 1995 bestseller, *Sacred Hoops: Spiritual Lessons of a Hardwood Warrior* (with Hugh Delehanty). The "Michael" he refers to is of course Michael Jordan.

> I flashed back to 1989 when I took over as head coach and had talked to Michael about how I wanted him to share the spotlight with his teammates so the team could grow and flourish. In those days he was a gifted young athlete with enormous confidence in his own abilities who had to be cajoled into making sacrifices for the team. Now he was an older, wiser player who understood that it wasn't brilliant individual performances that made great teams, but the energy that's unleashed when players put their egos aside and work toward a common goal.
>
> Good teams become great ones when the members trust each other enough to surrender the "me" for the "we." This is the lesson Michael and his teammates learned en route to winning three consecutive NBA championships. As Bill Cartwright [who played center on three of Jackson's Chicago Bulls' championship teams]

puts it: "A great basketball team will have trust. I've seen teams where the players won't pass to a guy because they don't think he's going to catch the ball. But a great basketball team will throw the ball to everyone. If a guy drops it or bobbles it out of bounds, the next time they'll throw it to him again. And because of their confidence in him, he will have confidence. That's how you grow."

Back when he was younger and cockier, Jackson admits, he would have quickly laughed at anyone suggesting that "selflessness and compassion were the secrets to success." But as he grew older and wiser, he began to view the world differently and forged his own collaborative, spiritual Type B vision of team building. Actually, it's so unique and idiosyncratic, you might call it Type J—for Jackson—but it's certainly at the other end of the spectrum from Type A. However you label it, no one's done it better.

Though Jackson's laboratory is basketball, he might as well be describing managing in a corporation. The qualities he focuses on—trust, confidence, selflessness, compassion, plus most importantly, getting rock stars with outsized egos and challenging personalities to work together for the common good—are exactly what you have to achieve when building teams in business. The basic dynamics are the same, whether you're herding cats for Apple, Alibaba, Walmart, or the Los Angeles Lakers.

When building teams for important projects, Type B managers need to be closely attuned to the strengths and weaknesses of the "players" they're assembling, and vigilant about the work's progress and how team members are getting along. Countless major projects are derailed not by lack of talent but by preventable interpersonal conflict. Will the team's participants mesh well together? Or will

---

"The Belonging Benefit"

Most employees much prefer to be part of a team they're committed to, rather than just a "member of an organization." Good managers promote *belonging*. They're adept at getting individuals of differing backgrounds, skill sets, and personalities to work together collaboratively. A team-building management approach that engenders esprit de corps is a key link in the productivity process.

---

they clash and cause discord and disruption—and drive the productivity train off the desired track?

If you're someone who can assess talent astutely, keep those independent feline personalities in line, and help them look outside themselves to find value in something greater, chances are you'll always have organizations vying for your management skills.

Management Insight

Much like cats, humans in a corporation, if left to their own devices, prefer to go their own way. An intuitive, inclusive Type B approach is helpful in understanding interpersonal dynamics and guiding team members to work together for the common good.

CHAPTER 8

The Best Managers I Knew Were Introverts

There's a popular fiction out there that management, especially senior management, is just a Type A extrovert's game. The stereotype that comes to mind is the über-confident executive effortlessly speaking to an audience of thousands, or skillfully mingling at events with mayors and senators and the like. Of course there's some truth to that. An extroverted personality does confer undeniable business advantages. But the fact is, introverts also make excellent managers—and senior executives. Their strengths are less obvious but no less effective. After all, don't Type B qualities like being quiet, thoughtful, and analytical feel like attributes that help you make sound decisions in a management role?

When I think back now on the hundreds of executives I knew and worked with, there are just a handful who come to mind as universally admired and respected. Oddly enough, all were quiet individuals who could easily be considered introverts—and all shared the same constellation of characteristics. They were:

Measured in their responses. Not prone to bursts of temper, but thoughtful in how they sifted through and processed information. They thus avoided a common pitfall of executivedom—going off half-cocked with an immediate, emotional Type A response when what is needed is a more carefully considered strategic one.

Highly analytical. Expert at finding their way through reams of data quickly and reaching the core of the matter. Though quiet, they were not at all indecisive—they just wanted to be sure they'd viewed an issue from all angles.

Good listeners. Being naturally quiet, they let others do most of the talking. But they were keen listeners. This brings to mind the first meeting I had, relatively early in my career, with a brilliant chief investment officer. To help myself prepare, I talked to a colleague about what I should expect. "He doesn't say too much," my colleague noted, "but he doesn't suffer fools very well." (With that as guidance, I tried hard to be extra well prepared, and less foolish than usual.)

Naturally risk averse. A critical management function is avoiding potentially disastrous risk. (Through mass amnesia, or something like it, a whole generation of managers seemed to forget about this in the years leading up to 2008.) One of those exceptional introverts I worked with was a chief information officer who had our organization readying systems for

Y2K many years before it became a national headline. We were all *completely* tired of the project by the time 2000 rolled around, but needless to say there was no drama when the big day came and went.

The voice of reason. Their voice was not the loudest but was often the most listened to. Tinged less with charisma than with rationality, it was heeded because people knew they had something reasonable and rational and thoughtful to say—which others respected and were eager to hear.

To be even moderately successful as an introvert in management, you have to be willing to force yourself out of your comfort zone. You have to be willing to make yourself get up and speak in front of lots of people, run large and contentious meetings, and wade into interpersonal conflict . . . when your natural inclination might be to go home and read *Anna Karenina*.

As we've seen, outstanding leaders come in all shapes and sizes and don't conform to stereotypes. Some of the inward-looking qualities that make people introverted also help them make excellent decisions—a critical element of what being an effective manager is all about.

Management Insight

The best managers make the best decisions, and the analytical introversion of many reserved Type B's can lead to sound decision making.

CHAPTER 9

The Difference Between Management and Leadership Is Overrated

Whether you're a naturally authoritative Type A manager or a more reserved Type B who has less expected but still highly effective management skills, I wouldn't blame you at all for being disturbed by the way management is often compared to leadership.

Admittedly, mine is a contrarian view. The leadership development business is a huge industry today—with "leadership" generally viewed as a visionary strategic pursuit—the high-minded endeavor of CEOs, senior executives, boards, and the like—while "management" is seen as the unfortunate stepchild mired in a myriad of dull operational details. Even my two favorite quotes on the subject betray a subtle bias.

> *Management is doing things right; leadership is doing the right things.*
> —PETER DRUCKER

I have nothing but admiration for Mr. Drucker, who arguably is to management what Freud is to psychology—the founding father and most original thinker the field has ever seen. Still, with all due respect, I'd humbly suggest that management too is about doing the right things. What decent, well-intentioned manager would contend otherwise? Would any thoughtful manager set out to do things wrong?

> *Managers think about today. Leaders think about tomorrow.* —ANONYMOUS

I'm not sure where this quote originated, but it comes up all the time in leadership training sessions. I like it for its conciseness and clear forward-looking orientation. But again, I feel it's subtly insulting to managers. What bright, conscientious manager isn't thinking to some extent about tomorrow?

Which brings me to the core of this chapter. No student of management would argue that there aren't massive differences between the role of a CEO and a shop floor supervisor—of course there are—but the differences between management and leadership are persistently and substantially overstated. The boundaries between the two fields are artificially constructed, and place far more separation between them than there ought to be. Simply put, the best managers are inherently good leaders—that's after all what much of this book is about—and, similarly, the best leaders are also excellent managers.

Let's consider this last point in more detail. The most effective leaders I had the privilege to work with over many years shared some prosaic qualities. They had an unflappable, solid Type B foundation that informed all aspects of their business lives and made others *want* to follow them. They were exceptional *managers*, in the literal sense of the word.

Let's review some of these Type B qualities that made them not only outstanding executives but also individuals who were both well liked and highly respected:

They managed time well. They were models of efficiency. They responded quickly to calls and messages, either personally or through their assistants. They were fast, direct communicators. Meetings they ran were always organized, often ending early. Time was a friend, not an enemy. One of the most revered executives I had the good fortune to know left promptly every day at 5 p.m. Of course he was at his desk every morning, quietly sipping coffee and carving through whatever reports and paperwork he needed to, before 7 a.m.

They managed risk well. They had a keen sense of where business danger lurked and what steps might be needed to mitigate it. Whether the issue was computer viruses or portfolios too heavy with securitized mortgages, they had a sharp eye for issues before they became crises. Sometimes protecting a business (how quickly we forget 2008) is more important than growing it.

They managed details well. Not bogged down by unnecessary details, they had surprising command of them, given the span of projects in their control. But they weren't prisoners of data. One senior vice president I worked closely with was known for her conciseness. "Summarize the issue for me in two sentences," she'd say. It forced you to organize yourself before opening your mouth. Not one sentence, not one paragraph, not an elevator speech—but two precise sentences.

They managed numbers well. Goes almost without saying, but their financial acumen was as natural as the air we breathed. "Know your numbers" was the simple three-word mantra of one executive vice president I reported to. Before any budget meeting with her, you'd best be familiar with all aspects of everything numerical in your purview—or you'd best not attend.

They managed people well. There was a common quality to their people management: They had high expectations but they treated people with respect. There was nothing "touchy-feely" about their managerial style, but it was built on a foundation of decency. They treated you as an equal who just happened to be in a subordinate organizational role. It made others not want to disappoint them—and instead want to do their very best.

They managed their own lives well. There's no perfection in life, and I can't pretend to know the details of their personal lives. But the way they conducted themselves at work, the balance they seemed to have between work and home, the personas they projected, gave the clear impression of solidity and integrity. As role models, they were easy to follow.

I always found it odd that I received more training—leadership development training—in the last five years of my management career than I did in the first twenty years combined. Because those early years, when I first moved into management, were the times when I really needed the training, not when I had two decades of experience under my belt.

Unfortunately, this dynamic—giving less training to those who need it more while giving more to those who need it less—is all too common in the management world. Yet there's no compelling reason why the practice of management should get short shrift when compared to that of leadership. The best management is at the core of the best leadership.

And for you many excellent managers out there, I have absolutely 100 percent confidence that you're doing the right things and thinking about tomorrow. On a day-in, day-out basis.

Management Insight

Whether they are a Type A or Type B personality, the best managers are excellent leaders, and the best leaders are excellent managers. The separation between the two fields has today become artificially vast.

CHAPTER 10

Evaluating Without Demoralizing

Conducting effective performance evaluations is like painting a room. If you do the "prep" work diligently—all the sanding, spackling, taping, and priming—the actual painting is easy.

Performance evaluations, performance management, employee evaluations, employee appraisals—they have different names in different organizations—can be one of the most stressful aspects of management. They can easily become a point of contention, a highly emotional "he said / she said" drama. Or they can be merely the final step in a logical, constructive, satisfying process.

There's some sentiment in management circles these days that traditional annual employee performance evaluations are useless—unsatisfactory and too often demoralizing, at best a blunt instrument for a delicate job. I'd argue that employee evaluations are one of the most integral but misapplied elements of management. After many years of using and receiving them, I firmly believe the problem is management itself—not the evaluation tool, but the way that tool is used.

Why is it in any way objectionable for managers to provide comprehensive assessments of how employees have performed over the course of a year? Isn't providing thorough, thoughtful feedback a key function of management?

Unfortunately, all too often managers aren't doing their jobs diligently, and in such instances problems with a formal evaluation just reflect broader problems of management. What kinds of criticisms of evaluations are most often heard? Here are two common ones: (1) Evaluations are too negative and critical—a litany of what you're doing wrong—they serve mainly to demoralize. (2) Evaluations aren't tough enough—managers duck or gloss over the needed, hard conversations.

Where do Type A and Type B managers often fit into this discussion? Not surprisingly, some hard-driving Type A's will naturally fall toward the critical end of the spectrum, providing employees a "litany of what you're doing wrong"—while more conciliatory Type B's will fall into the camp that would rather avoid nettlesome, confrontational conversations and tend to focus on a pleasanter review of "what you're doing right." Safe to say, from a manager's standpoint, there's little to be gained by being overly aggressive in evaluations, or by preserving cordial relations with an employee at the cost of candor.

As with so much in management, the most effective path usually lies somewhere in the middle, when executed honestly and thoughtfully. Evaluations are an inherently emotion-laden situation: For employees they're a report card on "how well you did your job." With this perspective in mind, let's look at ways for managers to make employee evaluations as constructive as possible:

Be candid about problems and generous when praise is due. This is pretty simple guidance: candor when needed and generosity when deserved. "Evaluating without demoralizing" doesn't mean the conversation should always be motivating and positive. Far from it. As we've discussed earlier, management without firm controls isn't management at all. Make no mistake—at the end of the day this is *your* evaluation of your employee. An effective appraisal should be an evenhanded accounting of results against objectives. It's also an excellent opportunity for Type B managers who are naturally inclined to be forthcoming with praise to provide it when hard-won results surpass expectations. For an employee who's given an outstanding yearlong effort, there's no point at all being emotionally stingy. Let the person know what a fine job he or she did and how much it is valued. Most importantly, an employee should understand where the comments are coming from. They should be fact-based and make good logical sense.

Maintain frequent communication containing meaningful feedback. To return to our painting analogy, this is the sanding and spackling phase. The best way to avoid surprising employees during an evaluation (which usually means the evaluation resembles a train wreck) is to communicate frequently and honestly throughout the year—a facet of management that usually comes easily for Type B's. How you do this of course is up to you. Personally, I found regular status meetings convenient and functional. In addition to providing the opportunity to discuss current projects, they were a place for immediate feedback, both good and bad, and no time for sidestepping problems. My preference was to hold weekly half-hour meetings for relatively new employees (or for veteran employees if there were issues to be resolved), and meet once every two weeks with employees who knew the job and were performing well. But there's no right or wrong as to frequency—whatever suits your business needs. And of course there's no point wasting valuable time in meetings. If everything is perfectly fine and there's nothing to discuss, just end the meeting after two minutes and get back to work.

Engage in a dialogue, not a monologue. The year-end appraisal is an excellent time for meaningful dialogue. This can be a time for Type B open communicators to shine. Significantly, it's also a chance for an employee to give his or her own perspective on many things: the job, the company, you as a manager, strengths and weaknesses and overall performance, ways to improve operations, and so on. It's a chance to step back and review the year from a high level: what worked and what didn't, and how things can work better in the future. Without exception, the best managers I've known were good listeners, genuinely interested in what their employees had to say. The very act of *being thoughtfully listened to* is a positive experience—an easy way to turn an event that's often perceived as one-sided criticism into a respectful exchange of ideas.

Make time for a (future) development conversation. A good way to wrap up the evaluation process on a constructive note is to finish by setting up a separate development conversation. This upcoming meeting will be a chance to discuss the employee's short- and long-term career goals, skills to acquire, opportunities of interest, mentoring possibilities, and so forth. It shows your sincere interest in the employee's future (which in itself, if perceived as genuine, goes a long way toward building loyalty). It's a tangible way to give the evaluation a positive, forward-looking orientation.

Of course the evaluation itself is only the tip of the managerial iceberg. The foundation, the infrastructure, on which an evaluation is based, should be built many months earlier. For a Type B manager who doesn't, shall we say, relish disputes and arguments, well-conceived employee job objectives are an invaluable asset, a manager's best friend, because if constructed properly, they provide a road map that can guide you and your team and will help ensure that employees are focusing their efforts where they should be. They provide a tangible scorecard at year end to see how actual achievements measure up, quite literally, against what was intended.

This is what Ken Blanchard refers to in his classic bestseller *The One Minute Manager* as "no surprises" management:

> "So is One Minute Goal Setting just understanding what your responsibilities are?" the young man asked.
>
> "No. Once we know what our job is, the manager always makes sure we know what good performance is. In other words, performance standards are clear."[1]

As they always should be. However, in the real world most managers spend a fraction of the time they should developing their employees' annual objectives. When one considers the uses to which these objectives will ultimately be put—the yearlong yardstick against which you measure your employees' overall performance, with likely compensation and bonus implications—it's easy to see their importance from a management standpoint. Yet busy managers often view annual objective setting as a bureaucratic exercise, a nuisance, a distraction—with other more pressing daily operational issues at hand.

Solid objectives help take the drama and uncertainty out of year-end performance reviews. (While some companies are moving away from traditional annual reviews, whatever the exact performance-rating framework they use, these organizations will in all likelihood still need some sort of evaluating, sifting, and sorting process.) Let's consider some typical hypothetical scenarios. Type A managers may find themselves embroiled at year end in a heated, contentious dialogue with an employee who feels he or she has performed considerably better than the manager does (a not uncommon situation). Or, with that same hypothetical employee, Type B managers may find themselves wanting to avoid that same emotional, angry discussion. In either instance, clearly measurable employee objectives can make such difficult conversations immeasurably easier. It's not you as a manager being hard or capricious or nasty or unreasonable. It's simply: *Here are the objective standards—how did your performance compare?* It's all very clear, recorded in black and white. It removes subjectivity and guesswork.

That's why they're called "objectives"—not "subjectives."

Let's consider five key components of well-designed employee objectives. They should be:

Clear. First and foremost, job objectives need to be clear. If objectives aren't clearly defined at the outset, it sets the stage for later problems. Absent appropriate clarity, when it eventually comes time to evaluate performance "he said / she said" situations easily develop.

Measurable. Job objectives should always be as specific and measurable as possible. Specificity helps remove subjectivity from the process. For example: *Respond to all client phone calls within fifteen minutes. Make ninety widgets a day. Tame three wolverines each month.* Regardless of the nature of the business, ensure that the volume of expected activity and the time of completion are readily measurable and clear.

Agreed upon. Objectives are most successful when employees are closely involved in the objective-setting process. A collaborative process, rather than a unilaterally imposed one, tends to promote employee engagement. This is not to say that employees get to decide how much work they do—managers are always the final arbiters of the goals that are established. But being closer to the actual work, employees may have more accurate assessments of how realistic certain goals are, and may have insights into more nuanced measures. There's also very practical value in having an employee take an active role in the goal-setting process. As a manager, you want your employees to have this added level of responsibility for their performance—skin in the game.

Meaningful to the organization. It's important that individual goals are not developed in isolation, but are closely aligned with broader organizational objectives. The most thoughtful job objectives frequently take time to develop, requiring back-and-forth dialogue among manager, employee, and senior management to ensure that effort is being expended in the right organizational direction. (There's no point spending time taming wolverines when what management really needs is antelopes!)

Ambitious yet attainable. As we saw with Dave's unfortunate example back in Chapter 4 on the importance of standards, it's critical that the bar be set at the right height. Set it too high and frustration and burnout result. Set it too low and you're not doing your job as a manager to optimize employee productivity. Ideally you want objectives that talented individuals *can* reach with strong, sustained effort.

For the Type B manager who wants to help ensure a successful and *drama-free* evaluation season, thoughtful behind-the-scenes preparation is key. To help with these preparations during the year, three simple questions you can ask yourself will let you gauge whether or not you're on track:

1. **Are your employees' objectives clear and are your employees fully aware of them?** As we discuss in detail in this chapter, it all starts with well-conceived objectives. These of course should be established and agreed to early in the year. Your employees' active participation in this process—skin in the game—is vital to eventual success. If objectives are easily measurable, well known, and transparent to the employee, that's a great foundation on which to build.

2. **Have your employees' results been well documented throughout the year?** It doesn't help if employee objectives are clear but nothing has been documented. Meaningful results should be recorded—especially for major projects—and be completely transparent to both manager and employee. Lack of documentation simply invites "he said / she said" disagreement between employee and management come evaluation time. Written documentation takes guesswork and subjectivity out of the process: *Here are the results—how do they compare to the specific objectives we earlier agreed to?*

3. **Have you provided consistent feedback throughout the year?**
   Was the entire chain of communication completed, so the results
   that were achieved based on the objectives that were set were
   duly communicated back and discussed? The operative phrase
   here is "no surprises." Your employees should have a clear sense
   of how you feel their work is measuring up against expectations.

It's a simple equation: If the answer to any of these three questions
is a resounding no, that's a red flag and it's time to try quickly to get
your managerial house in order—communicating with your employees and reviewing major objectives, results, and feedback . . . to at
least lay the groundwork before more formal evaluation processes
actually take place. But if all these steps have been diligently managed, annual evaluations should be easy and stress-free, more afterthought than drama.

Even in evaluations, authority takes many forms. You don't need
Type A intensity and a booming voice when you have logic and data
on your side.

Marcia, a first-year manager, was not looking forward to this
employee evaluation session. Henry, one of her direct reports, was
loud and outspoken, but he was also regarded as knowing the direct
marketing business well and had long been rated a top performer.
(Marcia felt that it probably didn't hurt that Henry had enjoyed a
longtime close working relationship with her predecessor, Ed, the
veteran manager who had retired.)

Now Marcia was planning to move Henry down a notch, from
"Exceeds Expectations" to "Meets Expectations," and she anticipated

Henry would put up a fuss. Which he did—immediately in the meeting. "How can you say I 'meet expectations'?" he protested. "I know more about this direct marketing operation than everyone else here combined!"

Marcia was by nature a relaxed and quiet Type B sort of person. She was logical and well prepared, two key reasons she'd been promoted into management. "No one's questioning your experience," she said deliberately. "You know I value it and rely on it. But look at your first and most important objective—the number of leads generated for our sales force. We both agreed on a figure of twenty thousand at the beginning of the year—an 8 percent increase over last year, ambitious but not out of line with prior increases. You ended the year at 19,600 . . . an increase over last year but still 2 percent below the target we agreed on in January. You know I have high regard for your knowledge of this business and the broader industry environment. But these lead-generating numbers that are core to your operation . . . well, they are what they are."

Marcia took a deep breath and waited for an angry onslaught while Henry went back over his own data. To her surprise, when he looked up he nodded and spoke more calmly. "Well, I suppose I understand," he said surprisingly quietly. "Guess it's kind of hard to argue nineteen six exceeds twenty."

If there's one key takeaway from this chapter, it's that most managers spend a fraction of the time they should optimizing employee objectives. When considering the long tail annual objectives have—tangible practical value over the course of an entire year—I always felt that a robust dialogue—maybe three or four drafts back and forth, and also including my own management at some point in the

"A Recipe for Confusion"

Circumstances change quickly in business, and there are many reasons why employee job objectives get out of date. But if your employees' objectives aren't accurate, how can you hope to evaluate your employees accurately? Following are common reasons why employee objectives—through no fault of anyone—need periodic checkups: (1) A major project is canceled. (2) A major new project is introduced. (3) A reorganization occurs. (4) The strategic direction of your organization changes. All of these things happen all the time in business, while employee objectives sit untouched and unchanged in a file—a recipe for later confusion.

process to be sure they "bought in" to the direction we were taking—was always well worth the time. I never once regretted it. I saw it not as a waste of time but as an *investment* of time—an investment in clarity and employee performance.

Management Insight

When it comes to employee evaluations, we have a tendency to blame the message more than the messenger. Well-planned evaluations, based on fair logical objectives, are actually an excellent opportunity to provide holistic messages that are candid, thorough, and motivating. This ability is one Type B managers excel at, and one others will find it valuable to cultivate.

CHAPTER 11

Small Things Make a Big Difference

"Think small." These two words, which also happen to comprise the most famous advertising slogan of the twentieth century (Doyle Dane Bernbach's longtime campaign for Volkswagen[1]), are anathema to business. The instinctive direction of the business world is outward. Growth, revenue, acquisition, market share—there's a natural tendency to think expansively.

No thoughtful businessperson would argue that big, visionary, strategic thinking is unimportant to an organization. But the fact is, in the day-to-day world of management, small things make a big difference. On shop floors and in office "trenches," where the vast majority of managers reside, the emphasis is on keeping operations moving, deadlines met, costs contained—"trains running on time." In this grassroots world, the nature of the manager-employee relationship is shaped less by weighty strategic concerns than by the myriad of small, moment-to-moment interactions that ultimately determine how an employee feels about his or her manager, and therefore the organization. This is the thread from which the cloth of employee engagement is made.

In this land—the world of small, which is highly populated— there are a number of issues Type A managers need to be watchful of, and a number of reasons why Type B managers are well positioned to be effective. Let's consider some.

There's a natural tendency for Type A's to be "on the go"—fast!— perhaps preoccupied by the "crisis of the moment" (a common state of corporate affairs). But in this peripatetic state, they may be oblivious to small oversights that can work against productivity. Let's take the experience of Robert as an example.

Robert was a vice president I reported to early in my career. He was smart, hardworking, an excellent, poised presenter, and a respected expert in Human Resources. He was also invariably twenty minutes late to his biweekly staff meetings. Suffice it to say, this didn't go over well. There were six of us on his staff, ambitious up-and-coming managers ourselves, and as soon as we realized this was a chronic pattern and we were on the wrong end of it, we didn't like it a bit. Consequently, we began to spend a good part of those twenty minutes each meeting talking about our tardy manager—joking, gossiping, grousing . . . generally complaining about him. Despite his solid skills, his career faltered, and in not too long a time he was relieved of the VP role and shortly afterward ended up leaving the company. Though I never knew all the details behind his departure, I always suspected that the casual thoughtlessness he displayed toward his own employees couldn't have served him well, and could only have contributed to his difficulties.

Keeping your employees waiting is viewed by many as a manager's prerogative. (After all, you're the boss.) But the costs of chronic tardiness are twofold: diminished morale and decreased productivity. In terms of morale, let's say it plainly: Employees don't like it. People don't like to be kept waiting. They get impatient. It breeds resentment. If you're the manager, it sends a clear message to your team that their time is not as important as yours: They're lesser beings with less important tasks, smaller planets orbiting a brighter sun.

In terms of lost productivity, just consider this chapter's earlier example. Six of us, middle managers all, earning reasonable salaries, were unproductively sitting around, doing little but complaining, waiting for the meeting to begin. In fact, as we'll see in the next chapter, time lost through unproductive meetings, taken in the aggregate, is a huge problem for business.

Net-net, there's no downside for managers being on time for their own employees. It's easy. It's respectful. It models good behavior. It saves money. And it's a small, simple way of showing employees you value their time and contributions.

Let's consider several more small arenas where a Type B sensitivity can make a positive difference in employee attitudes:

Return messages quickly. Like keeping people waiting in meetings, ignoring or not responding quickly to employee messages in whatever form—email, voicemail, text, note on a napkin—itself sends a message, but not a positive one. It says: "Your issues aren't that important to me." It also unconsciously models a message no manager knowingly wants to send: It's OK to keep people (e.g., customers) waiting—a position no conscientious manager could endorse.

Recognize small wins. Making progress, even a little progress, matters, and can be motivational. A thank-you or word of praise for something as everyday, say, as a meeting efficiently run, a client call quickly returned, or a nice concise memo can be effective. It never stopped surprising me how simple words of encouragement could boost employees' spirits when energy was flagging on a long, slow day.

Take a genuine interest in your employees. Not an excessive interest, of course, but a sincere interest, in their lives outside of work. There's a very practical reason for this as well. Outside factors shape inside performance. An employee with a stable, happy home life may be able to focus on work with a single-minded intensity that someone dealing with major problems at home may not be able to muster. This isn't meant as an excuse, just a variable for you as a manager to be aware of. The phrase "work-life balance" is heard a lot these days and has become a cliché, but long before we called it that it was still an integral aspect of on-the-job performance.

Marcia had worked for an intense, demanding manager for two years. Though he was difficult, in the end it wasn't his competitiveness or excitability or anxiety over deadlines that most bothered her. No, it was something much smaller than that.

Being a mature professional, Marcia could accept most of her manager's Type A workaholic ways. What really bothered her, though, was his habit, whenever she stopped by his office to ask him a question, of never taking his eye off his computer screen while he talked to her. He'd answer her questions adequately and carry on a cogent conversation—all the while seated with his back to her, resolutely multitasking.

"What drove me crazy," she said, "was that he couldn't take two

"When $3.25 Goes a Long Way"

I recently happened to be speaking with a young woman in a very good mood. She'd just gotten off her job at a hotel, greeting guests visiting for conferences—and at the end of the day her supervisor told her she was doing a really nice job and gave her a small card. The young woman showed me the card. It said: "We appreciate your outstanding service! Thank you for being so welcoming, thoughtful and friendly to our guests. Please enjoy a slice of pizza & a Pepsi for 75 cents as our thanks." At the bottom were listed local eateries where the card could be redeemed.

My initial reaction was to wonder (to myself) why she had to pay 75 cents—why weren't the pizza and Pepsi free? But no matter. And no matter that the card's value (let's assume in this part of the world a slice of pizza costs $3 and a Pepsi $1) was around $3.25. The young woman couldn't have been more pleased. The card was the highlight of her day. Of course the real reason she was so pleased had nothing to do with pizza or Pepsi or saving $3.25. It was the recognition she received. It was the simple gesture from her supervisor acknowledging she was doing well. The message was tangible and clearly communicated—and who doesn't enjoy a slice of pizza?

Over the decades I was involved in more employee surveys than I can recall. But one point I do recall is the one issue that came up in literally all of them—a chronic source of employee frustration: recognition. Employees never felt they were getting enough of it. This is ironic, because recognition can be so simple and inexpensive—unless you consider $3.25 a major capital outlay—yet so often overlooked. Why? The managerial dynamic goes like this: You're busy, you're frazzled, you have deadlines, meetings, many balls in the air and projects on your mind. You're under pressure and it's easy to disregard what may seem like the small stuff. But when you do take the time, even modest gestures have a surprisingly energizing impact. "My boss thinks I'm doing a good job," the young woman likely thought when she got home that evening. "I'll show her. Tomorrow I'll do an even better one."

minutes away from other work to look at me when he talked to me. It was like I wasn't important enough to him to do that."

Marcia's manager was a smart, hardworking, capable executive. When she mentioned this issue to him, he assured her it wasn't a problem—he could do both things completely competently at the same time. And indeed he could. But it came at a cost: her loyalty.

That's the management challenge with small things that "get under people's skin." They're so small they easily go unnoticed. Except by the employee who's acutely aware of them.

Management Insight

In the normal rushing about of a fast-paced work environment, it's easy to overlook "small things" that do in fact matter to employees. A Type B manager's awareness of these minor but not insignificant details can make a positive difference in employee attitudes and therefore productivity.

CHAPTER 12

Running Meetings to Increase Productivity, Not Profanity

How many times have you ever heard anyone complain a meeting was too short? (In four decades of meetings I never did.) But have you ever felt a meeting was too long? I'd say I did, oh, maybe 4 million times. Ever been frustrated at a meeting by rambling chitchat chewing up valuable time while work remains undone, or by stragglers who routinely wander in ten minutes late?

There are many places in the business world where Type B patience and thoughtful deliberation will be an unmistakable asset and will yield more productive outcomes . . . but running an efficient meeting isn't one of them. Meetings are the ideal environment for Type A's—in an entirely constructive way—to give in to their natural impulses toward, as Drs. Friedman and Rosenman put it, "a harrying sense of time urgency." But for you Type B's who have a natural tendency to collaborate and involve others, meetings are one place where too much cooperation and involvement of all parties can lead to a too-long, inefficient outcome. Meetings are one spot where impatience is a virtue. Thus, in the spirit of productivity, here are simple steps to help you run more efficient, effective meetings:

1. **Spend twice as much time on the agenda as you normally would.** One problem commonly afflicting meetings is unclear objectives. If you're not exactly sure what you're trying to accomplish, you can be sure it won't happen quickly. As meeting organizer, it's your responsibility to have clarity about what you're trying to accomplish. Consult with another team member if you need to. A little extra time invested at the front end will save more time at the back end.

2. **Spend twice as much time on the attendee list as you normally would.** Ask yourself, carefully: Do all of these people *really* need to be at the meeting? Or could some of them simply receive a brief email summary or quick call afterward? If you can reduce a half-hour meeting list by, say, four people whose presence isn't essential, that's two hours of productive time effortlessly returned to your company.

3. **Schedule the meeting for half the time you originally intended to.** Meetings are like accordions—they stretch naturally to fill the allotted space. If you schedule a meeting for an hour, you'll probably take the whole time, even if a fair amount of it consists of amiable, random off-topic conversation. In all likelihood if you schedule that same meeting for thirty minutes, you'll do what you need to in the tighter time frame. When I was in the corporate world, I routinely halved meeting times and was seldom disappointed. Try two-hour meetings at one

hour, one hour meetings at thirty minutes, and thirty-minute meetings at fifteen.

4. **Don't start late.** Way too much time is wasted on late arrivals. It used to make me crazy that certain people would be habitually late, thus regularly wasting some five to ten minutes for the entire group—and penalizing the punctual. The simple solution? Don't wait for latecomers. Start the instant you're scheduled to. Soon enough people will get the idea—no one likes to be embarrassed by straggling in during the middle of a cogent discussion. Do this a few times and you'll develop a reputation for promptness. I knew numerous (though not enough) managers who had hyper-punctual reputations, and they were respected for it.

5. **Consider—if it's appropriate for your business needs—holding a stand-up meeting.** I've seen data suggesting that stand-up meetings can be more efficient. Groups that were standing took less time to make decisions than those who were seated, with no loss in decision quality. For logistical reasons, stand-up meetings aren't always practical, but they're worth considering.

6. **Last but definitely not least: Do you really need a meeting?** Might there be other ways—a few phone calls, a couple of informal personal conversations, a memo to the team perhaps—that will achieve the same results as a meeting? There are plenty of times of course that you *do* need a full-on meeting, but it never hurts to impose the discipline of asking the fundamental question: Is this meeting even necessary?

"The Beauty of Brevity"

I've long been a fan of short. Admittedly, I have a limited concentration span. But in the business world, this can be an asset. The beauty of brevity is that time saved in one place is time—and labor—that can be deployed productively elsewhere. *Conciseness saves companies cash.* Consider a few extremely common activities besides meetings where brevity is your best friend:

Memos. Procter & Gamble for years was well known for a policy requiring employee memos to be no longer than one page. There's an old Mark Twain saying, "I didn't have time to write a short letter, so I wrote a long one instead." (Meaning of course that it takes more time to be disciplined, thoughtful, and concise than just to ramble on.) The shorter the memo, the better, so long as you cover what's needed in a clearly understood manner. Brief, well-conceived content also takes less time to decipher and read, thus saving time for the receivers as well.

Presentations and Speeches. How many corporate presentations or speeches have you attended where you came away feeling, "What a great presentation—*it was just too short!*" (Sorry, but I can't recall one of these either.) What's the easiest thing in the world for attention to do? Wander. Better for the speaker, better for the audience, better for the organization that gains productive working time (for perhaps dozens or hundreds or even thousands of attending employees) to keep presentations tight, concise—and leaving the audience alert and wanting more.

> Which has the additional benefit of providing more time at the end for Q&A and dialogue, usually a worthwhile audience-engaging exercise.

Some of these suggestions, like optimizing agendas and attendee lists, do require the meeting organizer—you, the manager—to spend additional time at the front end. But the organizational math is sound: Time saved in a meeting equals productive time returned to the company . . . and a little more time spent by one at the front end is preferable to a lot more time spent by many at the back end.

Management Insight

No one ever complains that meetings are too short. Well-prepared Type B managers who run good tight meetings will invariably be respected for it.

CHAPTER 13

Employee Development

Critical and Neglected

Old business joke:

CFO asks CEO: "What happens if we invest in developing our people and they leave us?"

CEO: "What happens if we don't, and they stay?"

It's hard to think of a key aspect of management that is more neglected than employee development: taking the time to help your employees broaden their talents and shape the future direction of their careers. Yet for a variety of reasons, this valuable activity is often ignored or handled as a bureaucratic exercise or afterthought.

One clear challenge for Type A managers, likely multitasking and heavily involved in day-to-day operations, is that this function has no immediate operational payback. It's a long-term investment in your employees, and while you may be rewarded with increased loyalty—no small benefit—it's also possible your employees will take their newfound skills and move on, as the above joke suggests, to another department or even company.

Despite the often more attentive people-focus of Type B managers, and the way this orientation would seem to naturally lend itself to such development activities, there's no guarantee Type B's will make employee development a high-priority function either. I know when I was in management I didn't spend as much time as I should have on the development of my own employees. I did spend some time, but in retrospect I see that I wasn't as consistent and thorough as I should have been, largely due to the same "no time to do it—we're struggling to do more with less" reality noted above. And no doubt it would have been helpful if during my career my own managers had spent more development time with me.

While some organizations excel at developing talent—G.E., for example, has historically been very well respected for its leadership development programs—research confirms that lack of development support is a widespread problem throughout the business world. One *Harvard Business Review* study, for example, focusing on young, high-achieving managers, found that insufficient attention to employee development led directly to retention problems:[1]

> Dissatisfaction with some employee-development efforts appears to fuel many early exits. . . . We asked young managers what their employers do to help them grow in their jobs and what they'd like their employers to do, and found some large gaps. Workers reported that companies generally satisfy their needs for on-the-job development

and that they value these opportunities, which include high-visibility positions and significant increases in responsibility. But they're not getting much in the way of formal development, such as training, mentoring and coaching   things they also value highly.

So why is employee development frequently overlooked? There are several causes, which in the too-busy world of management have their root in "too much to do in too little time."

Managers tend, for very pragmatic reasons, to focus most on the here and now. So many companies are in a constant state of upheaval—reorganizing, cost cutting, and trying to do more with less. In such environments, managers naturally concentrate most on essential day-to-day operations and less on longer-term activities that offer more uncertain payback.

There's just no time for it. A common but unpersuasive excuse. Even in an ultra-busy environment, there's always time for activities deemed important. Prioritize. If you believe employee development is a valuable managerial function, it makes complete sense to carve out the hours and minutes to support it. In retrospect, I know I could and should have done more.

Some employee development activities are done but not acted upon. In my years in corporate management, we did spend time trying to categorize and organize all of our employees into rather complex matrices, which were intended to be used for both development and management information purposes. ("Rock Star," "Diamond in the Rough," "Whole Lot of Problems," etc.—these are my own slightly fanciful versions of some of the many employee categories we used.) The problem was, these activities were perceived as so bureaucratic, confusing, and time-consuming that we managers were satisfied just to complete them and rarely did anything constructive with the data.

In addition to the reasons noted in the aforementioned *Harvard Business Review* survey, why is employee development planning a key function that makes good business sense?

People care if you take an interest in their future. Employee development is an excellent opportunity for both Type A and Type B managers. It's simply human nature: People are naturally well disposed to those who genuinely want to help them.

It builds loyalty, and loyalty increases productivity. There's a clear logical progression here. Taking an honest interest in your employees' future builds loyalty. Loyal employees are more engaged. Engaged employees are more productive.

Talented people want to advance, and appreciate meaningful support in the process. As shown by the *HBR* research, capable ambitious young employees want training, mentoring, and coaching. They want to acquire new skills. They want to become more versatile and valuable to an organization. Many years ago my employer invested heavily in my MBA, and it always meant a great deal to me. Who doesn't appreciate thoughtful support that helps them advance their own career? But the reverse side of this coin is, if one company doesn't provide this support, enterprising employees will look elsewhere for it.

One of the more unusual employee development situations I've experienced involved Jan, who was working in my department as a temporary employee in an administrative role. She was quiet, efficient, and capable, and as I gradually got to know her over a several-month period, I learned she'd lived for a decade in China, spoke fluent Mandarin, and had in fact opened and managed a chain of fitness centers there.

At that time the company I was working for was growing its international presence and was eager to expand into China—never a simple prospect, where a deep knowledge of the culture and local business customs is usually a prerequisite for any sort of meaningful progress. No matter that Jan's current role was in temporary administrative support . . . given her unique background it seemed clear that a connection to our international team should be made, and when I asked her if that introduction would be of interest to her, she told me in her quiet, competent way—yes, that would be fine.

I made an initial introduction to a member of our international team, and then quickly got out of the way. A dialogue between Jan and the group ensued, and within a matter of months she was serving on a consultative basis as a key member of our international delegation in China—a cultural and business advisor working closely with our top global executives and Chinese authorities.

It was quite the transformation—from a "temp" doing my filing and memos to a cultural liaison suddenly playing an important role in a Fortune 500 company's global explorations. Jan was a talented individual with a unique skill set. I couldn't have been more pleased for her.

All of which is a long way of saying you may be surprised by some of your employees' untapped skills.

Employee development activities don't have to be elaborate or costly. At its core this function is mostly a matter of managers taking the person-to-person time to understand their employees, recognize their skills and needs, and help them or guide them to fill in the gaps. But it's important to carve out the time to do this, to build it into your normal managerial routine, or in a busy schedule it will be easy to overlook or forget.

In this example with Jan, there was really never anything formal we did, it was just a matter of several casual conversations in which I got to know her better, learned about her background, and felt there could be a good fit with a need our organization had. If I'd never taken a few minutes now and then to have those talks with her, I'd never have known about her abilities. I'd have viewed her as a bright, courteous "temp"—not a Mandarin-speaking business builder.

Management has many challenges and frustrations, but seeing talented people advance because you were fortunate enough to give them useful direction surely isn't one of them.

Management Insight

Employee development is a widely ignored managerial function. Type B managers who take a personal interest in their employees and are attuned to their abilities will find the time spent on development activities an investment rewarded by appreciation and motivation.

CHAPTER 14

In Praise of Praise

One natural strength of the Type B manager is the tendency to connect well with others and be generous with praise. That's not to say all Type A's are parsimonious with praise, as there are of course many who will reward and recognize as quickly as anyone. But there's also a tendency for some Type A's to be so wrapped up in their work that they just don't take the time to provide that recognition. In the business world, praise is powerful and underutilized. From a management perspective, it requires minimal effort and no cost yet can be a highly effective motivator.

Recognition takes multiple forms. It can be monetary, it can be a formal performance-related program, or it can be simple words of praise or encouragement or a pat on the back from a manager. Companies tend to spend a great deal of time setting up often-complicated recognition programs. While these can be helpful, my own belief is what's really most needed is well-trained managers who provide praise, where appropriate, on a regular basis. Effective praise doesn't need to be elaborate or formal, just sincere. Frank is better than fancy.

Naturally praise shouldn't be dispensed carelessly when not deserved. That helps no one and only undermines managerial credibility. But in my experience, the business issue was hardly ever too much praise, but too little. Here are extremely simple reasons why it pays for managers to praise:

It costs nothing. Unlike many bonus programs, which can be highly valued by employees but have a huge price tag, the cost of verbal praise is always the same: zero dollars and zero cents.

It requires little effort. "Thank you." "Great job." "I really appreciated your work on that project." All of these take less than ten seconds to say. Maybe at most a couple minutes when you include some related follow-up conversation. (Again, my assumption is always that the praise is deserved or you wouldn't be giving it.) It's a modest investment of managerial time and energy that can pay significant dividends in employee morale.

It makes employees feel good. Always preferable from a productivity standpoint to have employees feeling good, rather than underappreciated and resentful.

When employees feel good, they work harder. Feeling valued is an effective motivator; positive morale raises energy levels right away.

Net-net, there's nothing for management to gain by withholding praise and recognition when it's genuinely warranted. One intriguing piece of employee research found that recognition is often a more powerful motivator than money.[1] More than 70 percent of survey respondents reported that their most meaningful recognition at work had no dollar value. While this dynamic may be less true at more senior levels where financial rewards steeply escalate, it's well worth bearing in mind at lower and middle organizational levels, where most employees reside and where the broadest productivity gains can be made.

Managing others is hard but not always complex. The praise situation is an unusually simple one. The fact that praise from management is so fundamental, with the benefits so greatly outweighing the costs, makes it surprising that individual managers and entire organizations get it so consistently wrong. As we've seen, multiple studies show that the single most important factor influencing employee engagement is an employee's relationship with his or her direct manager. Given this reality, the quality of that relationship is of crucial importance. However a relationship develops, and no matter the nature of the business, there's nothing for a manager to gain by being "emotionally stingy." It's in everyone's best interests to make thoughtful praise a key component of the managerial mix.

Management Insight

Well-placed praise is one of the simplest but most powerful tools managers have. Cost is small, benefits large. Type B managers who relate well to others are by nature well suited to provide praise effectively.

CHAPTER 15

Managing People
Who Are Hard to Manage

In the documentary movie *Buck*, there's a memorable line from Betsy Shirley, foster mother of Buck Brannaman, the real-life inspiration for the movie *The Horse Whisperer*. Betsy raised more than twenty children, resulting in a household that was at times, shall we say, chaotic. "Blessed are the flexible," she says with the conviction of one who knows, "for they shall not get bent out of shape."

In fact, this sentiment applies to management just as well as to child rearing. Managing challenging employees productively requires patience, intuition, and above all, flexibility—attributes many Type B managers possess.

Management would be the best job in the world, or at least one of the easiest, if all employees were highly motivated, unfailingly polite, always had a positive mindset, and were terrific collaborators. But of course they're not.

It can be a particularly challenging aspect of the role for some Type

A managers—likely highly motivated and disciplined themselves—to find the flexibility and patience to bring out the best in employees who may be so different from them. Perhaps the employees aren't too motivated, or are not really sure what they want to be doing in life, or lack a sense of urgency and commitment. Or maybe they're very bright and motivated—but also moody and stubborn. Or perhaps they don't collaborate well with others—or they collaborate too well and are chatty and easily distracted. I could go on (and on), but you get the point. And the fact is, they're employed by your organization—perhaps you hired them yourself—and presumably they do have the skills that enable them to do the tasks the job requires. (If they don't have the skills, then you'll be called on to let them go.)

Similarly, it can be challenging for Type B's to deal with the frustration, the confrontation, the need to stay right on top of a situation that needs staying on top of—when the natural inclination might be to take a hands-off *que sera, sera* approach and let things slowly resolve themselves over time. Unfortunately, when you're managing difficult employees and your own boss wants progress and results, unlimited time is a luxury you don't have. After all, business is business. And management—getting productive work out of others even if they're difficult—is what you're being paid for. This is where flexibility, being willing to view challenging situations in unexpected ways and course-correct when needed, will help Type B's with one of the toughest parts of the job.

I often felt this aspect of management was a variant of the old "80-20 rule" in business, in which 80 percent of your business is said to come from 20 percent of your customers. But when I was a manager, rather than 80 percent of my business coming from 20 percent of my customers, it felt like 80 percent of my time was spent on 20 percent of my (most challenging) employees. In this chapter we'll offer suggestions for working with various types of challenging personalities, including creative individuals and the growing army of employees with ADD/ADHD. And we'll start by providing ideas for managing employees who are talented, but plain old hard to manage:

Be thoughtful about assignments. To the extent possible, and naturally this isn't always controllable, depending on the nature of the work, try to match assignments well with interests and abilities. For difficult employees who are also quite talented—just difficult to work with!—try to provide especially substantive assignments that will utilize and stretch their considerable skills. "We give our best people the worst assignments" was how a colleague of mine used to jokingly put it. You may find that a well-chosen assignment can engage them and will bring out their best. An employee who's fully engrossed in a project is much less likely to go off track.

Make HR an ally. Despite Hollywood's tendency to humorously stereotype the meddling, bureaucratic Human Resources manager (and personally I thoroughly enjoyed Toby's portrayal on *The Office*), the fact is, when dealing with problem employees, HR can be an invaluable resource. They provide added perspective and (no small matter!) keep both you and the company out of trouble. Many sizable HR departments have specialists dedicated to helping managers handle serious employee relations problems. Don't hesitate for a moment to enlist their services if you feel you need to.

Be clear about your expectations, and what can and can't be tolerated. Confronted by any number of irritants— malingering, carping, gossiping, tardiness, interpersonal conflicts, work not turned in on time, or work of poor or mediocre quality—you need to make it completely clear what levels of work and behavior are expected, and what will and won't be tolerated. Clear annual performance objectives (see Chapter 10), coupled with ample real-time feedback when issues arise, are the managerial tools of choice.

Be clear about articulating pain points. Don't dance around problems—articulate the issues as precisely as possible. If there's difficulty, for example, with a certain member of your Badger Team collaborating constructively with members of the Grasshopper Team, state it. If an employee has problems delivering projects on deadline, state it. If a manager who reports to you is so demanding that he or she is burning out staff and causing too much turnover, state it. Then work with the individual in question to shape these current problems into future performance objectives.

Give ample feedback in both directions. Don't wait until midyear or end-of-year evaluations for feedback. Provide feedback often and in all directions—positive reinforcement when things are going well and corrective guidance when they're not. There's no way to course-correct if it's not clear that correction is needed—and naturally there's a difference between useful, insightful feedback and pesky micromanagement.

Don't feed drama. When conflicts arise, as they inevitably do, stay calm. Some challenging employees enjoy being provocateurs. Don't allow yourself to be drawn into the fray and pull rank and lose your temper, however tempting that might be. Prepare for a potentially volatile meeting by gaining tight control of your emotions going in. As the manager, you're the voice of authority and reason—maintain the moral high ground at all times. Remember, this is business, not a personal dispute—do your best to drain the emotion out of it.

Document clearly. As discussed in Chapter 16, on managing conflict, thorough documentation is a cornerstone of sound management. It provides necessary objective data when there are ongoing employee problems. Such documentation needn't be lengthy—a quick paragraph will do. It just needs to summarize clearly and concisely the issues that have occurred and why they're problematic. This data will later become extremely helpful for clear, fact-based evaluations, assessing objectively whether an employee's goals have been achieved or not. And it's essential should you need to build a case for an employee's termination.

Try to see things through the eyes of others. This is a circumstance where Type B flexibility and intuition serve you well. No one's perfect; all of us of course have faults. It's possible some of the fault in a fractured relationship with an employee is yours. Might there be something in your management style that's causing an employee to relate to you in persistently frustrating ways? Could such perceptions be valid? Occasional looks in the managerial mirror are always worthwhile—and often illuminating.

Engagement Challenges

In his book *The Art of Engagement: Bridging the Gap Between People and Possibilities* (McGraw Hill, 2008), author Jim Haudan does a fine job taking an employee-centric view of the grassroots factors that can impede employee engagement. Six chapters bear these revealing titles:

"I Can't Be Engaged If I'm Overwhelmed"

"I Can't Be Engaged If I Don't Get It"

"I Can't Be Engaged If I'm Scared"

"I Can't Be Engaged If I Don't See the Big Picture"

"I Can't Be Engaged If It's Not Mine"

"I Can't Be Engaged If My Leaders Don't Face Reality"

It's a nice, plainspoken summary of the challenges that employees and therefore managers face on a daily basis. Employee engagement is a fragile bond—hard to build, easy to disturb.

Recognize when it's time for up or out. A risk for many Type B managers—who naturally try to get along with others—is a tendency to put up with too much for too long. Unfortunately, persistent problems with employees rarely resolve themselves. At some point "enough is enough" and certain employees need to be managed, as the saying goes, "up or out." If a difficult situation has become chronic, with little sign of improvement, and it's consuming vast quantities of your limited managerial time, you may be at this point. At such times either employees raise their performance up or they find themselves out, looking elsewhere for work.

Know when to say when. When you know beyond a doubt that "up" isn't happening and "out" is, work closely with HR to follow all proper termination procedures. Then, as Nike would say, just do it. Make the move and move on. (See Chapter 17, on accountability, for more on letting employees go effectively.) Indecision erodes authority when firm action is needed. If a termination is capricious, it sends chills through an organization ("This could happen to anyone or, worse yet, me!"). But if a termination is unquestionably deserved, a manager will in all likelihood be respected for doing what needed to be done. Other employees usually know better than managers exactly what's going on in the trenches—who's a workhorse and who's a show horse—and problematic employees disturb far more than just their manager.

We'll turn now to an intriguing subset of the "difficult" employee population: creative individuals. Managing creative people isn't "hard" in the same way as managing the employees we've just been discussing—employees who are, say, unmotivated, oppositional, or stubborn—but it's challenging in that it takes an entirely different managerial mindset. And though I'll use some examples here based on my experience with advertising agencies, an unusually creative subset of the population, the fact is, managers will find creative individuals everywhere—from accounting to customer service to manufacturing to you name it—not just in classically "creative" environments such as advertising and marketing. Again, all of these are circumstances where Type B flexibility and intuition will serve you well.

One other key fact about creative types? No matter the nature of your business, creative employees can be extraordinarily valuable to you and your organization. They can come up with unexpected, brilliant solutions to intractable problems.

As the former head of national advertising for a Fortune 500 company (MassMutual Financial Group), I can tell you that over the years I had the privilege of managing many very creative people. I spent considerable time working with copywriters, art directors, TV commercial producers, directors, photographers, and designers, among others. It was both frustrating and rewarding, but mostly the latter. While creative individuals can be famously difficult—moody, introspective, overly sensitive, and so forth—they tend to be difficult in a very different way from the broader employee population. As a rule, they're also very motivated—highly invested in the artistic and creative challenges of the project at hand. So what does this mean for you as a manager?

Tell them what you want done, not how to do it. This is no place at all for a Type A manager to be overly controlling or autocratic. This highly creative portion of the population, more than any other, doesn't respond well to micromanagement or overly tight control. Client-imposed solutions are almost never optimal, and a heavy-handed approach seldom gets you where you want to go. It just breeds resentment. Better to provide a clear strategic road map (in the advertising business, for example, it would be called a "creative brief," a project overview developed by the ad agency with ample client input) and then let your creative employees figure out the best way to travel that road. They'll do a far better job themselves than would a less creative businessperson—like me—dictating a solution.

Lead with firm direction and a light touch. As a corporate executive I sometimes joked (mostly to myself—I didn't want to give anyone ideas!) that I could be flogged repeatedly so long as I was well compensated. Not so with highly creative individuals. Flogging—or even other, gentler means of corporate persuasion—is ineffective here. Creative people shut down under such circumstances, turn resentful, don't give their best effort. On the other hand, since creative teams often care deeply about the projects they work on, whether it's a new TV commercial or an "insane" new mobile device, you want to use that emotional investment to your advantage. In short, this is an excellent place for calm, thoughtful, strategic Type B guidance—plus praise is always welcome as a motivated team searches for the optimal solution. Creative teams respond well to suggestions, coaching, and encouragement so long as those suggestions are thoughtful and offered for consideration, not imposed. The one caveat here is that, whatever your business, this is never "art for art's sake," but art for commerce's sake. When a project is going off the strategic track—very cool but straying from your fundamental business objectives—it needs to be reined in. I was inclined to offer my creative teams a long leash but pull it in quickly when needed.

Don't just trust your own instincts and taste. The best example I can give of this involves a story about a TV commercial that almost never saw the light of day. An ad agency I was working with back in 2001 presented, as part of a new round of work, a rough draft of a proposed new TV commercial featuring a frog, a hot pink background, and loud, pulsating music by Joan Jett and the Blackhearts. I felt confident in my knowledge of the types of commercials that would work for a 150-year-old, appropriately conservative insurance company, and the way our customers would respond to them. So I did what I felt any rational advertising manager would: I killed the spot.

The only hitch was that we were about to leave for focus groups across the country, and at the last minute the agency's creative director asked me, would I really mind, as a favor to the creative team, if during the upcoming research we kept that crazy frog commercial in the testing mix. I could see that the creative team had affection for the spot, and there was no harm in doing a little extra research on it.

Over the next few days we conducted multiple focus groups with members of the company's target audience. The commercial in question, "No Prince Charming Required," showing the wild unpredictability of life (and therefore the need for life insurance) for a woman who never needed to kiss a frog, didn't just test well: It obliterated the competition. Women were inspired by it and men found it compelling. We ended up running it nationally for years, and it became the most successful TV commercial in the company's history, as well as the foundation for numerous seminars and marketing programs.

In the end, I was delighted my creative team hadn't listened to me. What did I know? I may not have been smart—but at least I was flexible. I listened carefully to people who had deeper experience in the field than I had, and then, even more importantly, I listened to our customers as well.

Last but not least in this densely populated Land of Challenge, we'll focus on those who have trouble focusing. If you've been in management for a reasonable length of time, it's a safe bet that at some point in your career you've found yourself frustrated by a talented employee who was undermined by seemingly *inexplicable but persistent behavioral issues*. It's also possible there's a specific reason for it. He or she may have ADD/ADHD.

This issue was first brought to my attention several years ago when I posted an article on Forbes.com on the particular challenges of managing difficult but very bright individuals. Several readers quickly contacted me and noted that the kinds of issues I was describing sounded as though they could well be related to ADD/ADHD (we'll get to clinical definitions in a moment).

In the busy context of normal day-to-day management, ADD/ADHD as a possible explanation for frustrating employee problems is an easy issue to overlook. I can speak from considerable personal experience on this one. Even as a Type B manager with a predisposition toward introspection and psychological approaches, while I was in management I never considered ADD/ADHD as an answer to puzzling employee challenges I faced.

But the more I researched the topic as Forbes readers contacted me, the more I was surprised to learn that despite the vast amount written about symptoms and treatment of ADD/ADHD, relatively little information was available about the implications of the condition for management. And the more I thought back on employees I'd managed over the years, as well as my own chronic disorganization, the more I realized I'd missed a multitude of clear signs. If many employees who have this condition have the potential to be highly productive but can be sabotaged by their own behavioral tendencies, what can you as a manager do to help these individuals succeed and be as productive as possible?

Let's first review some definitions and the problem's scope. ADD (attention deficit disorder) and ADHD (attention deficit hyperactivity disorder) are terms for a developmental disorder characterized by distractibility, impulsivity, and hyperactivity. ADHD is currently the clinically preferred name, though ADD is also commonly used. According to the American Deficit Disorder Association, approximately 4 to 6 percent of the U.S. population has ADHD. Even more concerning for the future management landscape is that at some point in their development, nearly one in five U.S. high school boys has been given an ADD/ADHD diagnosis, according to data from the Centers for Disease Control and Prevention—*a formidable number that will soon be entering the workforce.* And the condition isn't confined to the United States—it occurs worldwide. It's not just a disorder of attention; it affects impulse control, time-management skills, and goal orientation—all of which have negative implications for work-related performance. However, with awareness of the symptoms and issues that commonly result, plus some Type B flexibility and patience in working with these employees, there are clear tactical steps you can take to mitigate problems and help these individuals perform up to their potential.

How is ADD/ADHD often exhibited in a workplace setting? Since the condition involves a person's ability to become easily distracted and disorganized, it can cause difficulties in a structured, deadline-oriented workplace. (As the very words imply, a *dis*organized person will readily find challenges in an organization.) Simply put, it's easy for such employees to go "off track." That's when you need to get them back on track by focusing on specific areas:

Time management. ADD/ADHD has a clear impact on time-management skills. Becoming easily distracted can interfere with the timely completion of tasks, and there's a tendency for people with ADD/ADHD to underestimate how long tasks will take. Thus, more frequent check-ins from managers, or computer-based reminders, for example, can help keep projects moving at the desired pace.

Office configurations. Because of the ease of distractibility for these individuals, open office arrangements with few walls or dividers to filter out conversations and other noises may lead to problems. To the extent practical within your own particular business setting, more privacy and quiet are helpful to keep someone with ADD/ADHD focused and on track. Again, management flexibility—as opposed to "this is the way we've always done it here"—can make a positive difference.

Reward systems. Since these employees' attention easily wanders—the essence of the condition—a manager may want to use rewards, either tangible or simply verbal, more frequently than normal. Even small rewards can have a positive motivational impact, and can help employees with ADD/ADHD stay focused during lengthy projects.

Team dynamics. Effective collaboration, as we know, is always a valued attribute in the business world. Individuals with ADD/ADHD are generally active, lively talkers—but even too much of a good thing can be a problem—and excessive chatting or socializing can lead themselves (and others) off-task and prove disruptive to team activities. Though there are of course exceptions, employees with ADD/ADHD tend to be more effective in individual contributor rather than team leader roles. It also makes good sense when working with these people to give especially careful thought to a team's composition, and to be cognizant of ongoing interactions among team members.

Closer supervision. One broad implication for managers of employees with ADD/ADHD is the need for somewhat closer supervision than you'd normally provide—to help ensure that projects stay on the right course in the right time frame and that the needed results are achieved. To the extent possible, you'll want to be thoughtful about how assignments are made, bearing in mind the particular strengths and weaknesses of the individual.

In short, an intuitive Type B approach can be more effective than a "my way or the highway" style when dealing with these not uncommon issues.

It should be noted of course that it may not be immediately apparent whether an employee has ADD/ADHD. This may or may not be information an employee chooses to share with a manager. However, this section and the suggestions in it are meant to be food for thought about a growing problem; they may stimulate conversations and ideas for management strategies. You should also be aware that certain medications can be very effective at normalizing ADD/ADHD symptoms, though this is naturally a matter for physicians and their patients to discuss.[1]

One final point that is worth emphasizing: Over the years some of my most chronically disorganized employees were also among my most creative and talented.

They were extraordinarily valuable to our organization.

Management Insight

Effectively handling all kinds of difficult personalities is unquestionably one of the most demanding aspects of management. Maintaining a flexible, intuitive approach, both strengths of Type B individuals, is a constructive way to address this challenge that all managers face.

CHAPTER 16

The Fine Art of Managing Conflict

I once had a mentor who was in many ways a classic, old-school Type A executive—authoritative, decisive, somewhat excitable but, most important from my standpoint, utterly honest and direct. I respected him and his judgment. One day we were discussing my future, my executive potential. "I'll tell you," he said in his forthright style, "you're bright, you have an MBA, you're hardworking, you have integrity—these are all good qualities for management. But I just don't know if you can handle conflict. Frankly, I don't know if you want to handle conflict. I don't know if you have the stomach for it. Because so much of management, particularly at the higher levels, involves dealing with conflict on a regular basis. Can you see yourself doing that?"

I always remembered that conversation. My mentor was right in that I never really did come to enjoy conflict. Most people don't. But I did, over the years, recognize it was a vital part of the job, and developed strategies that helped me deal with it.

Effectively managing conflict is one of the hardest parts of management. No doubt about it. As every manager knows (or it's an exceedingly lucky one who doesn't), conflict abounds in the workplace. Over the years I dealt with so much of it I used to call it the "currency of management." Indeed, the ability to handle conflict well can distinguish a successful manager from one who is unhappy and ineffective in the role.

When faced with conflict, Type A and Type B managers are apt to have very different strengths—and weaknesses. Being innately more assertive and authoritative, Type A individuals generally have an easier time confronting conflict directly, while reserved Type B's are more apt to try to avoid it. The reverse side of the conflict coin, however, is that in wading right in and perhaps imposing a "my way or the highway" solution, some Type A's will alienate people in the process, while Type B's may well tend to look for a collaborative solution acceptable to all parties.

The fact is, even if Type B's don't seek conflict, temperamentally they're surprisingly well equipped to deal with it. Conflict situations are inherently emotional and combustible. High-voltage Type A personalities can be the spark that ignites an unstable environment. Quieter, emotionally unflappable Type B's can help keep things calm and lead the way to de-escalation and constructive resolution.

Let's get more specific. What are common causes of workplace conflict? Looking back over my own career, I recall conflicts with employees over issues including salaries, promotions, recognition, evaluations, relations with other team members, concerns about being managed too much and about not being managed enough, projects that were too tough and projects that were too dull, reorganizations, downsizing, mergers . . . and once in a while someone who was for no discernible reason plain old insubordinate. In short, just about everything. I never liked conflict. But I realized early on that if I expected to advance and be well compensated for management, doing my best to deal fairly and directly with conflict was a critical piece of the job. Accordingly, here are suggestions to help you bring order to the chaos of conflict. A structured, rational approach can make a stressful part of the job less so.

Accept the inevitability of conflict in management. Just recognize that it's part of the job, in fact a significant part of the job. Don't waste mental energy ruminating about it and wishing it weren't so. Don't feel bad you feel bad about it. Accept it for what it is: It comes with the managerial territory. As a Type B, if you can get past not liking conflict, you may realize you're surprisingly adept at handling it.

Don't be a conflict-avoider. As we've said, conflict avoidance is a natural tendency of many Type B's. But difficult interpersonal workplace problems won't disappear if you ignore them; they'll only fester and worsen. Chronic conflict-avoiders end up losing the respect of their employees, as well as their own management. You can't simultaneously be a conflict-avoider and a highly effective manager. It's just not possible. But by forcing yourself to face conflict, you may find yourself getting used to it. As the saying goes, competence breeds confidence.

Stay calm. In the midst of a heated conflict situation, remaining calm is a challenge for anyone. Even when you're provoked, keep a close hold on your temper. Stay as calm as you possibly

can. There are some memorable lines from the famous Rudyard Kipling poem "If":

If you can keep your head when all about you
Are losing theirs and blaming it on you . . .

Kipling wrote this in 1895. Though it wasn't written for business, I always felt there was management relevance in the
message. If you can keep your wits while everybody else is
acting slightly crazy . . . well, that's an outstanding position
to manage from.

Maintain the moral high ground. Remember, *you're* the manager. You're in charge, you're supposed to be the voice of reason.
Don't lose control or pull rank or cede the moral high ground.
Calm control is always an advantageous demeanor. If you as a
manager are not the voice of reason in a dispute, then who is?

Work closely with Human Resources. Part of HR's role
involves dealing with employee relations problems. My
management approach was predictable: In delicate, volatile
situations, get all the help you can. (More details on this subject
can be found in Chapter 23, "Get Help When You Need To.")

Document meticulously. When serious conflict occurs, as a
manager you need to keep accurate records of it. This is
essential. During employee performance appraisals, for
example, you need clear documentation to avoid discussions
dissolving into foggy "he said / she said" disputes. And when
it's necessary to terminate someone, you of course need

detailed documentation—again, a time to work closely with HR—to be sure the organization avoids legal exposure. Adequate documentation is an integral part of management.

Don't think in terms of "winning" so much as constructively resolving. A manager's role is not to "defeat the enemy" (even though it may feel that way at times), but to elicit optimal performance from the area he or she is managing. Accordingly, best not to leave wounded bodies in your wake but to resolve conflicts fairly and expeditiously, and move forward as constructively as possible. Get closure and move ahead—the sooner, the better.

Here's another way to view conflict, another perspective on it that can help you keep it *in perspective*. Many "crises" at work aren't really crises, they're "situations" that have been blown out of proportion. In all likelihood no one's hurt, no one's sick, no one's in danger or dying. Yet, real or not, many work situations are quickly elevated to crises and make many people just as anxious as if they actually were.

Most work crises are manufactured, based in perceptions more than objective facts. Now and then you'll encounter a legitimate work crisis that has the potential to do serious harm to you and likely a lot of people. I encountered a couple of those over the course of my career, but here I'm not talking about those. I'm talking more about things like: The wild man in the C-suite is really, really angry today because sales are 0.7 percent below target this quarter, or the tiger lady in the corner office is about to explode because her PowerPoint didn't come out exactly the way she expected it to and the board meeting is in an hour.

These types of situations, of which there are approximately 2 million corporate variants, often involving tightly wound Type A executives with impulse control issues, are by no means enjoyable, but they don't really deserve to rise to the level of crises, with the widespread rise in mass anxiety implied.

So what do you do if you're caught in the vortex of a faux crisis? This is where your innate Type B calmness, your relative tranquillity, can come to the fore. Several suggestions:

Start by counting to one hundred by threes. This is just a distracting and delaying tactic. Get your body in hand first and the mind will have the best chance to follow. Get control of your breathing, blood pressure, and pulse. That's job one: Get and stay physically calm.

Find that perspective. As noted above, most work crises—not all of course, but many of them—are overblown and likely driven by executives (I know because I used to be one), with no human beings in imminent danger and no serious damage about to occur. Given this view of reality, it becomes important for those caught in the moment to find that accurate perspective. What *really* is going on here? Is this situation one that should induce mass anxiety, or is it actually more of a frustration, a minor problem—eminently fixable—that has been amplified by personalities and a business culture accustomed to elevating anxiety levels on a regular basis? So if you can try to gain the perspective to see things as they are rather than the size they've been magnified to, that's a very positive step.

Try to be the voice of reason. If you cultivate the ability to stay calm and look for reasonable constructive solutions at these moments—let's figure out a quick fix for that Power-Point, let's examine the broader competitive sales environment, etc.—you'll find yourself respected for it. You may even gain a reputation as a go-to person in such situations, which is not at all a bad reputation to have in business. The world of calm as opposed to crazy: As we've discussed, this is where unflappable Type B's have a serious natural advantage. You'll also find that simply staying calm yourself has the added benefit of making others calmer.

I once asked a friend exactly what made Mariano Rivera such a great relief pitcher. My friend considered the question for a moment and then said thoughtfully, "He doesn't have a pulse." Meaning of course that Rivera was able to stay preternaturally calm in what is widely considered a wickedly stressful and highly public environment—closing out a professional baseball game—and was able to routinely come up with peak athletic performances because of it. (Of course his wickedly cut fastball didn't hurt either.)

Aspiring to Mariano Rivera's level of sangfroid is a tall order for anyone. But if you as a steady Type B manager, of stable mood and temperament, can bring a more structured approach to workplace "crises," trying to find a more rational than emotional way into problems, that's an excellent place to start—and a valued quality to bring to the workplace. Distraction, perspective, reason—all are effective crisis containment tools, especially if a crisis really isn't one.

There's one last aspect of conflict that's important to recognize: While conflict is usually unpleasant, it's by no means all bad. In fact, it can be the pathway to something better. Here are some tangible upsides to it:

You learn a valuable life skill about dealing with disputes. As a manager, as we've seen, conflict is so prevalent that you can't do your job effectively without confronting it. And there's a useful carryover to life outside management. How many personal relationships founder on conflict that is unexpressed, ignored, or handled explosively? Learning not to avoid conflict but to manage it constructively pays dividends well beyond the business environment.

Dirty laundry gets aired and (at least sometimes) cleaned. Conflict among individuals and teams forces contentious issues into the light of day. Rather than festering below the surface, where subtle grievances and bad will can undermine both personal performance and group dynamics, conflict that is openly aired has at least a chance of being resolved, which is usually a better outcome for all parties than lingering resentment.

It can spur innovation. Constructive resolutions of workplace conflict can become a pathway to improvement. Workplace studies have concluded that increased innovation and improved performance can be one of the substantive benefits. This isn't completely surprising, as open workplace conflict produces bursts of activity, and increased activity *can* yield innovative results.

Worst enemies can end up best friends (or at least colleagues who speak to each other). The best way I can illustrate this is anecdotally. As a manager, I developed what I thought was a nice collaborative Type B tactic: When personal conflicts between two individuals on my teams became too intense, I gave the two of them free lunch passes and forced them to have lunch together. No one else could be present, so all they could do was spend time together, face-to-face, and hopefully speak and communicate. I only did this a few times, but results were generally positive. In these situations conflicts were diminished, and the involved employees became civil colleagues if not exactly BFFs.

It would be naïve not to acknowledge that conflict can be painful, destructive, disruptive, and costly to individuals and organizations. But if we view conflict as an inevitable element of human interaction, and we attempt to constructively manage it rather than avoid or eliminate it, that's a first step toward making its considerable energy work for us, not against us.

Management Insight

Handling conflict effectively is one of a manager's most challenging and critical roles. Once Type B managers overcome their natural tendency to avoid conflict, they may find themselves surprisingly adept at handling it.

CHAPTER 17

Standing Firm on Accountability

Accountability—holding your employees responsible for achieving the results that are intended—is, not entirely surprisingly, a critical skill for managers. Holding people accountable isn't as simple as it may seem. It involves conflict and confrontation. It involves applying pressure. It means closely managing projects you may not feel like closely managing. But it's a key thread in the fabric of management.

I recently spent time with a *Harvard Business Review* study that summed up the situation nicely, if provocatively. Its headline was: "One Out of Every Two Managers Is Terrible at Accountability." It went on to describe how 46 percent of high-level managers were rated poorly on the measure "Holds people accountable—firm when they don't deliver." Another study, from Towers Watson, a well-respected compensation and benefits consulting firm, noted that 24 percent of companies responding to their survey awarded bonuses to employees "who fail to meet even the lowest possible performance ranking."[1]

In short, being perceived as too soft on accountability is both a widespread management shortcoming—and most definitely not a reputation any effective manager wants to have. No manager wants to be seen as weak. So what exactly is going on here, and more importantly, how can you avoid becoming one of the unfortunate 46 percent?

Firm accountability can be more natural for Type A's than Type B's, for whom that air of managerial authority may not come quite as easily. But given the data we've just described and the universal nature of these issues, there's more than enough trouble with accountability to cut across personality types. So let's look at things you as a Type B manager—especially if you have a tendency to retreat from enforcement situations—can do to be part of the solution rather than the problem:

Recognize that effective accountability becomes easier to achieve when you have strong employee objectives to back you up. Too many managers (and I saw a considerable amount of this myself) regard establishing employee objectives as a tedious annual exercise rather than an important business activity. If the standards by which performance is to be measured aren't well conceived and clear, how can you hope to hold people accountable to them? Clear standards beget clear management.

Recognize that these same objectives are the key to holding accountability discussions that are rational, not emotional. This is the ultimate payback for managers of well-conceived employee objectives. If these objectives are meaningful and measurable, then many aspects of managing—from daily operations to year-end evaluations—become a rational, not emotional process. As we first discussed in Chapter 10 ("Evaluating Without Demoralizing"), are these clear and hopefully agreed-upon standards being met? If they are, great. But if they're not—and this should be simple to determine, given their metric nature—well, that's a problem you need to candidly address. Different organizations, of course, have different employee evaluation arrangements. But it matters less if evaluations are formal or informal, or annual, semiannual, or quarterly, than if employees' objectives are clear. Then at least you have a reliable accountability yardstick, an opportunity to make performance-related conversations fact-based and rational, not subjective and emotional. Little is more frustrating and inconclusive than a heated performance-related dialogue with an employee when there is not data to back up either of you. Your employee may be genuinely convinced he or she did a great job, and you may be convinced the employee did a poor job. But neither of you can prove anything. You might as well be, as a colleague of mine used to say, "wrestling with a cloud."

Don't be afraid to diplomatically question dysfunctional compensation policies. Notice I say "diplomatically" here, as you never want to overstep your managerial bounds. But on the other hand, if you work for one those 24 percent of companies that are paying bonuses to failing performers (as mentioned in the aforementioned Towers Watson study), that's fair game to question. Simply put, it makes no business sense. I managed for more than two decades in an incentive compensation environment, with the features of our compensation plan changing with some frequency—but one constant was that never once were failing performers awarded bonuses. All that does is reward behavior you don't want to reward, while potentially alienating those employees who in fact are doing excellent work.

Have the discipline to not duck disputes. Holding people accountable when their results or behavior are not up to expected standards will sometimes involve conflict. Employees may not agree with your assessment of them. That's why many managers prefer to look the other way even if they instinctively know that's the wrong thing to do. Interpersonal conflict is unpleasant. Unfortunately, dealing effectively with unpleasantness—and constructively resolving it—is part of the role of management. So take a deep breath, look the conflict squarely in the eye, and acknowledge that handling such situations is integral to what you as a manager are being paid to do. When you can regularly and successfully address these matters without secretly wanting to run in the opposite direction, you're mastering the difficult but crucial art of accountability.

Model the right behavior yourself. When you as a manager are visibly holding your own direct reports accountable, this sends a powerful leading-by-example message to others in the organization. There are no favorites here. This is how the game is played. They may think: If senior management is doing this, we certainly should be too.

Accountability drives productivity, and productivity drives results. The integrity you show as a manager by fairly but firmly holding your people accountable will earn you respect from both management and employees in your organization.

The ultimate in accountability is having to fire people, having to terminate their employment because they're not doing the job satisfactorily—for any number of reasons.

If it's any consolation, no one likes to do this. But let's assume that for reasons of talent or performance or effort or behavior or cultural fit—or whatever unfortunate issue—you as the manager have determined that a certain employee has to go. How do you go about it in the best possible way?

Again, recognize that this *is* one of the most painful aspects of management, especially when you have to fire someone you've had a close working relationship with and genuinely like and respect. This is hard for everyone—Type A or Type B—and may be especially wrenching for some of you gentler Type B's, who would much prefer not to put another human, particularly someone you like, in an unemployed predicament.

To which I'd just add: You have to change that way of thinking; you have to lose that mindset. If you want to succeed in management, this is part of the price you have to pay. If you can't bring yourself to fire someone when it needs to be done, you're in the wrong job.

Also, to clarify, I'm making a distinction in this chapter between an individual firing and the mass terminations that occur during large-scale layoffs. While those large layoffs of course are never easy either, there's a different dynamic that occurs when dozens or hundreds or even thousands of people are being shown the door. There's less responsibility for the individual manager. But for the always challenging world of individual terminations, here are tips to help you make a stressful undertaking less so:

Never go off half-cocked. This is no place for impulsive Type A action or anger or decisions in the heat of the moment—this is instead a time when a measured, controlled Type B approach will serve you well. Among other things, mishandled employee terminations can often have serious legal and financial consequences. It's always a place for a thoughtful, well-planned course of action.

Document meticulously. Be sure that significant past problems with the employee in question have been diligently documented. This is naturally something you as a good manager should have been doing all along whenever substantive issues occurred. If this hasn't happened and your records are sparse, it may be best to wait if you can until more problems take place, and then carefully document those, so all your "ducks are in a row."

Work closely with Human Resources. HR, if they're doing their job well, will help ensure all the necessary ducks are in fact there, and will help you follow an appropriate process. Their objective counsel can save you, and your organization, from your too-patient Type B self. For decades I worked extremely closely with HR on delicate employee matters and never for one nanosecond regretted it.

Security. You'll want to be sure your company's security operation (some, in larger organizations, are much more sophisticated than others) is kept informed, and perhaps avail-able if needed, when the actual termination takes place, and that corporate assets and data are safeguarded. Though these preparations may sound excessive, depending on the circum-stances and personalities, firing an employee is an emotional, combustible, unpredictable event. All may go smoothly and quietly or chaos may result. You want a difficult situation handled fairly but with minimal drama. Think risk mitigation.

Beyond the logistical planning is the actual delivery of very hard news. What should you keep in mind?

Communicate with candor and clarity. Professionalism is the order of the day. Be well prepared. Know what your message is going to be and stick to it. There's a reason why this particular employee didn't work out. It's not a time to hide behind email, or to ramble or be overly emotional. Be concise, clear, and—most important of all—emotionally prepared for the moment.

Empathy. How your message is communicated makes a real difference. Genuine empathy matters. Having been on both sides of these conversations, I can attest that being treated with respect and dignity matters. Ask yourself: How would *you* want to be treated if you were receiving this message?

Employees on the shop floor know better than anyone who's an excellent employee and who isn't. If a firing is undeserved, you've got a problem on your hands. But if a firing is truly deserved—if an individual simply can't do the job or has had a corrosive influence on an organization—the vast majority of hardworking employees will recognize what needed to be done and will respect you for it. Type B's take notice: Excessive managerial inaction when corrective action is needed only breeds disrespect. No one wants to be perceived as a "weak" manager. Firmly and fairly holding your people accountable is an integral part of the job. It's what you're paid to do.

Management Insight

A well-liked Type B manager who effectively holds his or her employees accountable will be a well-respected Type B manager. Without firm accountability, management can't achieve the results it requires.

CHAPTER 18

The One-Word Key to Effective Delegation

While most everyone would agree that delegation is critical to managerial success, how often are you dissatisfied with the results of what you've delegated? How often is the "product" that is returned to you not exactly what you hoped for? While this is sometimes the fault of the person completing the assignment, it's often the fault of the person giving the assignment. And there's a common root to the problem. One word sums it up: *clarity*. (Or lack thereof.) While those executing an assignment have the responsibility to deliver a professional product, those making the assignment have the responsibility to ensure that the assignment is, as an old friend of mine used to put it, "clear as a mountain crick."

If you're a Type B manager who casually throws a project out there, sees where an employee takes it, and has faith all will end up well, you have a responsibility to make sure the person with the assignment knows exactly what he or she is expected to do. Good delegation is a great time-saving talent. As we've noted, no less a business rock star than Warren Buffett has a reputation as such a keen—and doubtless effective—delegator that he's been called the "Delegator in Chief."

Let's dissect the delegation process. Following are areas where it commonly goes astray:

Clarity of assignment. Is an assignment as clear as it ought to be? Let's consider an imaginary example: Your boss (as most managers of course have their own bosses too), quite possibly distracted, edgy, harassed by too much to do in too little time, calls you and says, "I need a quick competitive analysis of Barking Dogs of America." We'll assume Barking Dogs is a powerful rival that has been gaining market share at an alarming rate. "The board's expressed an interest in it and so has Schnauzer [your CEO]. It's high priority. I've got to run to a meeting now, but I want you and Beagle to handle this. I know I can count on you both—trust me, there's a lot of interest in this one!" How will you respond to this phone call and assignment? Your answer will be something along the lines of a jaunty "Sure, no problem—you can count on us. Beagle and I are on it!" But what exactly are you and Beagle on? Does your boss want a paragraph? A page? Slides? A twenty-page report? And analysis of *what*? Sales? Earnings? Market share? Distribution? Advertising? All of the above? Who knows? All you really know is that the project is important and your boss is anxious.

Clarity of responsibility. I can't tell you how many times in my corporate career I was given assignments for "me and Beagle" to handle. Or worse still, "me and Beagle and Spaniel," three trusted lieutenants. Even if you and Beagle and Spaniel are all very capable, which no doubt you are, whose assignment is it? Who does what to whom? Without a clear project *lead*, what you've mostly been given is a recipe for confusion.

Clarity of time. Let's return to our hypothetical canines. The request was for a "*quick* competitive analysis." Well, how quick is quick? Could it be a day? Maybe. A week? Possibly. Two weeks? Conceivable—a competitive analysis can get pretty meaty. What both you and your boss most want to avoid is a phone call just, say, three hours later with your boss barking, "Where's that competitive analysis? I'm meeting Schnauzer in ten minutes!" (When you were planning to meet Beagle over coffee first thing tomorrow morning to discuss how you'd approach the project.)

Clarity of communication. So often what is intended to be communicated by one person is not actually what is perceived by the other. Too many times projects founder on the shoals of faulty communication. So how do you prevent delegation-related problems from occurring? From a manager's perspective, a key element is to make sure there's ample time when a substantive assignment is given (no harried phone calls from distant airports, please), and to follow a clear assignment with a message like:

> If there's anything at all you don't understand about this Barking Dog project, just let me know. I don't mind at all. I'd much rather you check in with me now if I've been

at all unclear, or at any point in the project, preferably earlier than later, if you need more direction.

No question is a bad question—just ask.

There's no guarantee you'll end up with precisely what you want, but you *can* improve the odds.

Clarity also has value well beyond delegation. In fact, you may have noted that this quality, in one form or another, comes up repeatedly in these pages as an integral part of the managerial process. It's easily overlooked, but without it, uncertainty reigns. Employees are unsure of roles, assignments are misunderstood, time is wasted, priorities are muddled, and operations run inefficiently. The quality isn't top of mind but a bit subterranean. Clarity is like a lubricant that helps the engine of management run smoothly. Without it, management just doesn't work well at all.

Being more decisive and forceful, Type A's tend generally, though not always, to be more on the clear and definite side. Type B's, who often see things in shades of gray, possess a subtlety of mind that can at times translate to fuzziness. While clarity is always desirable, that doesn't mean its pursuit is an invitation to micromanagement. It means it always makes good business sense for employees to understand what is expected of them.

Beyond unclear delegation, lack of clarity takes many forms. Let's consider several areas where it's crucial to effective management:

Clarity of priorities. The best managers at any level, from CEOs to on-the-floor supervisors, are clear communicators.

They leave no doubt what's important and what's not—what needs to be done and when. As a manager, how many times have you been frustrated by direction that was unclear, or by a department or division or CEO that just didn't know where it wanted to go? The best managers are clear thinkers, clear speakers, and provide clear direction and feedback. If anything is unclear, it's understood that no question is a bad one.

Clarity of performance expectations. As we discussed earlier, in Chapter 10, most managers spend only a fraction of the time they should working closely with employees to set performance objectives that are clear, agreed upon, and measurable. Annual objective setting is too often treated as a tedious bureaucratic exercise when it's actually a vital management function. Well-designed employee objectives will help guide work activities for many months to come.

Clarity of behavioral expectations. As with performance expectations, it's always good for employees to know exactly how they are expected to behave. While behavioral issues may be a non-issue for highly motivated top performers, over the years some of my most talented and valuable employees occasionally did have substantive problems collaborating with others (aka "teamplayerism"). Unfortunately, when a behavioral issue surfaces, it can quickly become an emotional situation— plus an all-consuming devourer of your management time.

Clarity of vision. While management is sometimes said to be focused on the business of today and leadership on the business of tomorrow—a sentiment I disagreed with in Chapter

9—individuals in both roles need clarity about where they want their business to go. Think of Steve Jobs, with his meticulous total attention to the Apple product experience . . . or any anonymous but respected line manager who knows his or her department's business cold. No matter the size of an operation, you need a clear vision of what success looks like.

Uncertainty in business is the enemy of accomplishment. Clarity can be overlooked as an essential managerial ingredient because it's often just taken for granted. We *want* to believe our management knows its stuff. But anyone who's been on the wrong end of unclear direction knows you can't go far without clarity. Or actually you can. But probably not in the right direction.

Management Insight

Clear direction is like a lubricant that keeps the management engine running smoothly—without it, it's easy for employees to go off the desired track. For Type B managers, ensuring a delegated project is completely clear can make all the difference in receiving the results they expect.

CHAPTER 19

Trust and Respect

Warren Buffett, always legendary for his integrity, in a letter to his Berkshire Hathaway shareholders once said this about trust:

> After some other mistakes, I learned to go into business only with people whom I like, trust, and admire. . . . This policy of itself will not ensure success: A second-class textile or department-store company won't prosper simply because its managers are men that you would be pleased to see your daughter marry. However, an owner—or investor—can accomplish wonders if he manages to associate himself with such people in businesses that possess decent economic characteristics. Conversely, we do not wish to join with managers who lack admirable qualities, no matter how attractive the prospects of their business. We've never succeeded in making a good deal with a bad person.[1]

Given the overarching importance of trust in all relationships, business and personal, it's surprising how often it's absent in management-employee relationships. Trust is the solid floor on which the emotional framework of the manager-employee relationship is built. Without this strong foundation, a relationship is unsteady at best.

Why is trust between employee and manager in chronically—and unnecessarily short supply? Honesty knows no personality type, and there's no single simple answer to this question, but there are identifiable high-level factors. When I think back to my years in management, several broad themes recur:

Disingenuous communication from management to the rank and file. Lack of credibility erodes trust faster than you can say "rightsizing." Employees have finely honed "spin detectors" and excessive spin seldom yields the intended results.

Modeling behavior employees don't fully respect. While leading by example should be, as we've noted earlier, foundational, leaders have been known, shall we say, to not always demonstrate the actions they expect of others.

Financial pressures that force managers into actions they'd much prefer not to take. Truth is, whether one is a harder-edged Type A or a softer-styled Type B, no manager enjoys reducing staff, trimming benefits, cutting bonuses, and so forth, yet these actions are often the inevitable consequence of weak business results. Tough circumstances force good people into difficult decisions. In these hard times, employees' future trust in their leadership will be determined by *how* things are done (e.g., with transparency and candid explanations, as opposed to minimal or dubious communication). It's worth noting that issues like communication and behavior are within an individual manager's power to control, whereas financial pressures may at times be uncontrollable.

As a reasonably typical Type B manager myself, I recognized that it was critical for my employees to trust me if I expected them to be fully productive on my watch. They had to be willing to do their best, without trust issues getting in the way. For the most part I believe I was successful in this, yet I know there were times I lost employees' trust, and even failed badly. Let's consider a few examples:

- I lacked the backbone to support someone who deserved it when she was faced with arguably unfair political pressures within the organization to dismantle a successful marketing program she'd built. In this instance my desire to avoid conflict—a tendency I was often able to overcome—was a mistake. Trust in my leadership was an immediate casualty.
- Management systems such as forced rankings (aka "stacking") put me in a position to deliver performance messages, and employee rankings, I sometimes didn't completely believe in. Yet I had to deliver them, since that was my management role, which I understood, accepted, and was fairly compensated for. Such messages were invariably detrimental to productive employee relationships. Which meant trust in me diminished. (As I've noted before, no one claims management is an easy job!)
- Employees occasionally had unrealistic opinions of their own performance or behavior. For this, there's a relevant old saying: "There are no guilty people in prison." In such cases I never

regretted losing someone's trust, as I was simply doing what I completely believed the job required.

Even with the best of intentions there are innumerable ways trust can be undermined in the business world—and, once lost, it's hard to regain. An employee will naturally think: "This person betrayed my trust before—why should I believe he [or she] won't do it again?"

In short, trust is a fragile but exceedingly valuable commodity in management. It can make all the difference between an employee who is engaged and highly productive and one who is disengaged and even destructive.

Let's turn now to a related quality, a cousin of trust if you will, that also plays a key role for managers: respect. While this statement may initially sound counterintuitive, it's my considered opinion that friendship has no place in management. But haven't I been making the case on many of these pages that the formation of positive employee relationships that Type B's in particular excel at is a key element in the management process? Yes, absolutely true, and though the bond of friendship is one of the greatest things in life, my long-time belief as a manager is that *close friendship* best stays outside the management suite. Respect, not friendship, is what a manager needs.

Why is respect so valuable? It's an underrated quality that fits as perfectly in the world of management as a well-tailored suit. Let's examine why:

People naturally want to do their best for those they feel respected by. There's nothing complicated about it: Employees respond well to being treated well. It puts them in a favorable productive mindset. As goes the old military saying, which is also the title and subject of Chapter 24, "Take care of your people and they'll take care of you."

People resent not being respected, and a resentful attitude is never conducive to productivity. Employees are always highly attuned to subtle messages about the level of managers' respect. When that level indicates something less than genuine appreciation and respect for an individual, that's an unmistakable message—with significant negative long-term implications for that individual's attitude toward the job at hand.

So why is it important that this bond of respect not seep over and cross the line into deeper friendship? While this discussion may seem basic, the fact is, in a close working relationship there's a natural tendency for friendship to develop between manager and employee. And while a solid working rapport between the two is always desirable, and helps drive strong performance, when that rapport crosses over into close friendship, it can quickly compromise your ability as a manager to objectively exercise control and firmly take charge of a situation when you need to.

Over the years I've experienced and observed this dynamic at all levels of management:

New managers. There's a natural tendency for new managers to want to be liked by their employees. To some extent this is fine, as it's preferable to an overexuberant exercise of new authority, which almost certainly will be resented, especially if the new manager has formerly been the employees' peer. But if a new manager thinks he can be a pal and relate to coworkers the same way as in the past, that notion will collide with reality as soon as tasks go a bit off track, and control or correction needs to be exerted, or performance appraisals need to be done. Additionally, such manager/employee friendships can lead to perceptions (and realities) of favoritism, which naturally is antithetical to fair management. In short, a mindset shift needs to take place for new managers to be genuinely respected and ultimately successful in this new, more authoritative role.

Seasoned executives. At the highest levels of an organization, while relationships between seasoned executives and their direct reports are naturally somewhat different from those at more junior levels, the basic dynamic remains the same. There may be decades of shared history, and if a manager—in this case perhaps a leader of an organization—becomes too close a colleague and friend to a subordinate, when substantive business problems arise, as they always do, this friendship has the potential to impede the leader's ability to make tough-minded judgments and decisions. If it doesn't, and the leader remains as objective and firm as he or she should, in all likelihood this will deeply strain or fracture the relationship. Once again: You can say many things about management, but rarely can you say it's easy.

The solution, though not the execution, is simple: Diligently maintain a certain professional distance. Build rapport and gain respect from your employees, but maintain a boundary between those feelings and real friendship. This takes emotional discipline. During my years in management I genuinely *liked* many of the employees I managed. But when I let those feelings of liking someone

"Why Management Transparency
Is Good Business"

A key element of trust is credibility. Do your employees believe what you say? Are your—and your organization's—actions consistent with your words? Credibility counts—which is why I was pleased recently to come across a study showing the practical, not just ethical, value to an organization of management transparency. Such transparency, implying consistently candid and open management communication, is often viewed by management as "nice to have" but from some perspectives impractical and even naïve when dealing with constituencies as potentially contentious as employees and shareholders.

This study, conducted by a firm in the employee engagement research business, shows the positive role transparency plays in maintaining an engaged workforce.[2] The key finding? *Management transparency is the top factor when determining employee happiness.* (In the context of this survey, "employee happiness" was defined as a concept very similar to employee engagement.) Suffice it to say, employees in a positive mindset are more committed to an organization and therefore more productive. Based on more than forty thousand employee responses, the research found an unexpectedly strong statistical correlation between management transparency and employee happiness.

I'd never seen a connection made so directly between how management communicates and how employees respond to it. It removed transparency from the more nebulous realm of "ethics" and gave it practical business value.

Yet that's only logical. People like to be dealt with honestly. They appreciate it and respond well to it, just as they quickly sense disingenuous and opaque communication. *If I can believe and trust my management, the study affirms, I'll work harder for them.*

drift over into deeper friendship, I know I was a less effective leader, with resulting difficult and painful encounters when I had to do what the role required. On the other hand, when I maintained more emotional distance, when I simply had rapport and respect, it was easier and ultimately better for all parties involved.

Management Insight

A Type B manager's impulse to form close, positive working relationships is an excellent one. If these relationships evolve into deeper friendships, however, it reduces objectivity and undermines a manager's ability to do his or her job effectively when difficult situations arise.

CHAPTER 20

The Performing Arts

Ken was a middle manager in Marketing who was easy to overlook. A quiet keep-to-himself Type B sort of fellow, he was regarded by his own managers as a solid enough employee but unremarkable, a reliable tactician but certainly not someone who was "going places." Unbeknownst to everyone at work, because of his natural shyness Ken had taken up stand-up comedy as a hobby. He found performing gave him confidence, and it surprised him, once he grew accustomed to it, how much he actually enjoyed being on stage in clubs, in the spotlight, making people laugh. One day, about six months after he'd begun to feel comfortable with his comedy routine, Ken had to make a presentation to senior management. A key competitor had suddenly pulled out of West Texas, providing a possible opportunity for Ken's company to move in with a sizable advertising presence.

The senior management team was prepared for a dry, factual, probably rather boring fifteen minutes, and was not at all expecting what unfolded. Once given the floor, the quiet middle manager seemed transformed: Ken spoke with poise, energy, confidence, and touches of humor. He knew his material well and moved around the room confidently—several of the senior managers realized immediately that he in fact was a far better presenter than they were! Ken gave a flawless presentation, persuasively making the case for increased advertising, and finished with a flourish, walking over to the company's CEO, leaning on the table, looking him in the eye, and directly addressing him: "Now, I ask you, does this feel like the kind of opportunity we as a company can possibly afford to miss?"

Ken received the West Texas advertising funding, but more importantly, he was never again viewed the same way in the organization. His career accelerated; he was moved onto an executive fast track. "Why was I never aware of him before?" the CEO wondered. "What an extraordinarily capable young man!"

In fact, Ken had always been capable, but no one had noticed. In his breakout presentation to senior management that day, it wasn't so much what he had said but how he had said it: with complete self-assurance and aplomb, in the limelight.

Whether it's giving a presentation, running a meeting, or speaking more formally to a large audience, what I call the corporate "performing arts" are an integral part of every manager's career.

Three things I can say with certainty about public speaking: (1) Most typical, quiet Type B managers start off fearing it (studies have shown it's only slightly preferable to losing a limb). (2) It's one of the most valuable business and career skills you'll ever have. And (3) it's a skill that most importantly and most definitely can be learned.

Of the universe of outstanding public speakers and presenters, a few are just born that way. Give them a stage and a microphone and they can talk a dog off a meat wagon, as the saying goes. The other 99 percent of us, however, have to work at it.

Fortunately, the work isn't that hard and can be extremely rewarding, assuming you're motivated to improve. Full disclosure: There are a lot of ways to skin this cat. There are a legion of companies out there—many excellent—that teach public speaking to people all the time. I'm not one of them. I'm just a quiet person by nature who, over time, gained a functional knowledge of speaking and presenting because I realized it would be helpful, indeed essential, to my career. So what I'm not passing along is a system that can work for everyone, but simply four insights—nothing profound or difficult—that proved valuable to me, and I believe can be of value to other Type B managers—and some Type A's as well.

1. **Watch yourself on video.** I first did this for five minutes many years ago at a public speaking seminar given by my employer, and it was the wisest five minutes of my business time I ever invested. It wasn't pretty. On video I could see right away what needed to be improved. I was technically proficient in that I knew my subject matter (in this case it was advertising), but I needed to be far more animated, emotive, engaging. The video was a clear, unforgiving road map showing me quickly where I needed to go.

2. **Find your own style that you're comfortable with.** Know who you are, and what your strengths and weaknesses are. Being understated by nature, I was never going to be a fiery Type A speaker who'd pace around a stage like a panther and enthrall thousands with "fire-and-brimstone" emotion. But that was no

excuse to be boring. Two things I *could* do reasonably well were use dry humor and tell stories. Those were natural aspects of my personality that could be integrated into my public speaking. That's a great thing about speaking and presenting—there's no inherently right way to do it. You can be charismatic, motivational, educational, entertaining, informative, low-key, professorial—you name it—whatever works best for your personality.

3. **Pick out one person in the audience and pretend you're having a conversation with that person.** This is by no means an original insight, but a practical tactical maneuver I especially liked. It can help turn a potentially overwhelming situation into a manageable one. Instead of facing dozens or even thousands of people, you're (sort of) having a personal conversation with one other person. Naturally over the course of a speech or presentation, you can focus on numerous different individuals—but focusing on them one at a time is a helpful way to cut a large, inchoate event down to size.

4. **Practice, practice, practice—know your material cold.** For me this was by far the most important element—there's no substitute for thorough knowledge of your topic. Get completely comfortable with your content. Facing a large audience is the absolute worst time to discover that you're really not too sure what you want to say. If you're preternaturally gifted, perhaps you can bluff it, but for most of us mortals this is a recipe for implosion. Personally I never liked to memorize things—I'd end up sounding too wooden—but I wanted to clearly understand and think through all aspects of my message. When my

kids were growing up, I'd spend hours before a big presentation practicing quietly in our basement, with the ironing board as a podium, and in the car driving to and from work. It was a classic "competence breeds confidence" scenario—putting in the time made all the difference. My performance could vary from bumbling (if I hadn't prepared well) to effective and even entertaining (if I had).

Like Ken at the beginning of this chapter, I was not a natural public speaker, but I became a whole lot better than when I started. You can too.

Management Insight

The ability to speak persuasively to an audience is a tremendously valuable management skill. It's also a skill that definitely can be learned by even the most reserved Type B manager—even if you feel you have no natural talent in that direction.

CHAPTER 21

The Joy of Feeling Valued

Shortly after retiring from the corporate world, I received an email from a former colleague who had recently changed jobs. "I haven't worked this hard in years and have never felt so valued," she wrote. "What a strange combination. I learn something new every day and am only worried my brain won't hold any more information. I'm exhausted by Friday and it's just great. Who knew?"

To me, by far the most important phrase in this uplifting note was "and have never felt so valued." I can say with certainty that if my friend had just changed jobs, was working harder than ever, and felt totally unappreciated, her experience of this new position and the tone of her comments would have been entirely different. "I haven't worked this hard in years and have never felt so unappreciated" might have been the content of an alternate communiqué. "What a combination. I have to learn something new every day and am worried my brain won't hold any more information. I'm exhausted by Friday. Who knew things would turn out this way?"

As we've seen, taking the time to communicate openly and forth-rightly, especially when the intent is positive, is a clear strength of the Type B manager. We also know an employee's relationship with his or her direct manager is the single most important factor in employee engagement. And a key component of a productive manager-employee relationship is invariably the employee feeling valued for the work that is done. Without that feeling—when employees start to lose the sense that the product of their labor is valued by others—motivation quickly wanes.

Providing this sort of assurance is an innate ability many insightful, empathetic Type B managers have. It can be a difference-maker, at times allowing employees to accept lower compensation or longer hours or more of the inevitable frustrations that accompany difficult tasks than they otherwise might have—because they feel their diligent efforts are recognized and appreciated. Time after time in business I observed how small gestures of appreciation and encouragement could change attitudes from disgruntled to pleased (or at least OK) in the blink of a manager's eye.

The management implications are clear. This isn't an invitation to abdicate good judgment and managerial authority. Naturally appreciation shouldn't be tossed out casually when it's not genuinely felt or deserved. But when it is deserved, there's nothing for a manager to gain by withholding it.

If you value an employee, let him or her know it. If you don't make that explicitly clear from time to time, your employees may well not realize it, even if you think they do. Sincere words to that effect cost nothing and can make the difference between disengagement and productivity.

There's a wonderful saying from the late, great author Maya Angelou:

"The Surprising Power of Common Decency"

Common decency isn't one of the qualities that often come to mind when we think of the tools managers have at their disposal. Yet over the years in management I observed its power on many occasions. Employees who were treated decently were much more apt to "go the extra mile" for their managers than those who were not. Common decency—certainly not restricted to one personality type but a quality many considerate Type B's have in abundance—thus made good managerial sense not because managers wanted to be well liked, but because it was effective.

Since management, as we've seen, is all about achieving results through others, it's only logical that people want to do more for those they're favorably disposed to. Yet employees become accustomed to working for "bosses" who routinely overstep their authority and treat subordinates with something less than the respect they'd wish for themselves. Depending on the company and its managerial culture, it may come almost as a pleasantly motivating surprise to be treated thoughtfully, as an equal, albeit in a subordinate organizational role.

Common decency is a quiet, unassuming attribute, communication in a minor chord, rarely discussed in management textbooks and MBA courses. But as you quickly learn on the shop floor, it's a valuable managerial quality. It gets positive results.

"People will forget what you said, people will forget what you did, but people will never forget how you made them feel." I don't believe Ms. Angelou had business in mind when she wrote this, but she might as well have. It has full relevance for management.

······················· **Management Insight** ·······················

Genuine appreciation for tasks well done is an essential element in the management mix, one that thoughtful Type B managers are well positioned to provide.

CHAPTER 22

Self-Awareness

All Managers Need It

"How would you experience your actions if you were on the receiving end?"

These thirteen words, from the book *Leading with Intention: Every Moment Is a Choice* by Mindy Hall, sum up for me, as well any single sentence can, one of the most crucial aspects of successful management.[1]

Clear-minded cognizance of how other people perceive you is fundamental to leading them. Without it, one is essentially "flying blind." Possessing realistic self-awareness also represents an opportunity for reflective, inward-looking Type B managers, who have realistic perceptions of their own strengths and weaknesses, to lead effectively. Employees naturally respond well to people who have accurate, not grandiose, ideas about their own ability. Self-awareness isn't one of those big marquee leadership qualities like vision, charisma, strategic thinking, or the ability to speak eloquently to an audience the size of Tulsa—but it's a quieter, ancillary quality that enables the high-octane ones to work. Simply put, it's a psychological catalyst.

Over the years I saw many careers—especially at higher management levels—derailed by lack of self-awareness. Individuals felt they were omnipotent and they took unwise risks, or didn't recognize when actions that felt authoritative were actually demoralizing. And they generally didn't have an accurate "read" on how others were decoding the messages they were sending. On the other hand, the most effective executives I knew had realistic assessments of their own abilities—their strengths and weaknesses, their effect on others, the personal gaps they needed to fill.

It's always pleasant—if rather uncommon—to find out something that you've long intuitively believed has been validated by research. This was the case when I came across a study emphasizing the importance of "self-awareness" as a critical trait for successful leaders. The study, "When It Comes to Business Leadership, Nice Guys Finish First," examined seventy-two executives at public and private companies with revenues from $50 million to $5 billion.[2] Some of its findings resonated deeply.

> Leadership searches give short shrift to "self-awareness,"
> which should actually be a top criterion. . . . Interestingly,
> a high self-awareness score was the strongest predictor
> of overall success. This is not altogether surprising as
> executives who are aware of their weaknesses are often
> better able to hire subordinates who perform well in cat-
> egories in which the leader lacks acumen. These leaders

are also more able to entertain the idea that someone on their team may have an idea that is even better than their own.

As we've seen earlier, the qualities commonly associated with Type A managers, such as being decisive, forceful, and controlling, if not tempered by a high degree of awareness as to how they're being perceived by others, can easily frustrate and alienate those on the receiving end. At the other end of the spectrum, Type B managers, if not sufficiently self-aware, can have a tendency to slide into inaction and complacency—an approach that will likewise hinder effectiveness.

So how should companies use this type of data? Predicting management success, particularly when one is hiring from the outside, is always a tricky business. (More on this subject in Chapter 28.) The self-awareness study concluded: "Companies and their investors need to put more effort into evaluating the interpersonal strengths of potential leaders. They should focus more on *how* a leadership candidate does the work, and not focus exclusively on *what* he or she has done. . . . However, there are limits to the degree to which an individual can improve his or her basic ability to interact well with others. This means that focusing on interpersonal skills when selecting the right candidate becomes critical."

The self-awareness research summary also commented that "soft values drive hard results." That's a nice way to put it. Soft values like self-awareness are no substitute for traditional skills like maintaining authority and driving for results—without those you probably won't get out of the starting blocks—but they're a very valuable complement for the long run.

Management Insight

An accurate view of yourself and your environment is integral to management success. Without it, you'll always be flying blind, lacking a compass. Type B managers who know their business and have a realistic perspective on their strengths and weaknesses are well positioned to lead effectively.

CHAPTER 23

Get Help When You Need To

This subject is so basic and intuitive I'm always surprised it's not discussed or written about more. When you're dealing with a delicate management problem, and the solution is not at all obvious to you, where should you go and what should you do?

The excellent news is, even if you're a keep-your-own-counsel sort of Type B manager, whose natural inclination is to work things out on your own, in the business world there's never a need to work in isolation. If you're part of an organization of any size, help is every-where. Get it. Get perspective on a difficult employee problem from someone in your company (or outside it, if that's where your closest colleagues are) whose judgment you trust and respect. This could be anyone: a mentor, your own manager, a colleague, an old friend, or a contact in Human Resources. During my years in management I went to all of these people at different times to seek opinions when employee issues arose. It isn't a sign of weakness. It's sensible judgment.

I found Human Resources unfailingly helpful, and I made a point of establishing close working relationships with individuals—regardless of rank—who I felt were especially capable. I never for a moment regretted it. Let's consider ways Human Resources operations can be helpful when you're facing challenging management problems:

Difficult employee situations. Of which there are many. As any manager knows. Disgruntled employees, disputes between employees, compensation matters, recognition issues, downright hostile employees, and so on. It's management's role of course to constructively resolve such situations. When conflicts got too nasty or emotional or tangled or confusing, I never hesitated to call an HR colleague to help me sort things out—or at least provide a needed neutral perspective.

Firing. There's an old saying, "Any lawyer who represents himself has a fool for a client." To which I'd add, "Anyone who fires someone without working closely with HR is a fool as a manager." As we discussed in Chapter 17, terminating an employee without proper protocol and documentation can place an organization, and even you as a manager, at legal risk. If HR is doing its job, they'll ensure that all appropriate steps are taken and all ducks are in a row. It may take a little longer, but it's far preferable to finding yourself on the wrong end of a damaging lawsuit.

Development planning. Good managers develop employees; they look out for their careers. Employees appreciate such genuine interest, and it can pay off in higher levels of engagement and productivity. HR was a useful resource in this regard. At various times they located training opportunities for me and alerted me to in-house employees who could be good additions to my team, as well as suitable departments for team members who might do better in new surroundings. At one point they helped arrange a maneuver in which another manager and I simply traded employees (a "straight player swap," as they say in the sports world), and it ended up working out well for both individuals and teams.

The need for a sounding board for all manner of management issues. I tried to develop close working relationships with several individuals in HR whom I knew and trusted, and who knew me and the functions and individuals I managed. Then, when issues arose—they could be anything (a training seminar I was looking for, an angry employee, a problem with a vendor)—I'd just pick up the phone. Basically they became readily available, free, valued consultants. Sure, I realize there was a salary cost to our company, but providing such management counsel is part of what HR staff is normally paid to do.

To make the abstract more tangible and add texture to this topic, let's get more specific about the kind of delicate employee issues where an outside perspective may be warranted. To be sure, the number of situations that can challenge a manager is virtually infinite. Here are three (of many) from my own management experience where the opinions of others proved invaluable:

Inappropriate executive pressure. Early in my management days I was told by my own manager, a VP, to give a lower

year-end evaluation to an employee than I believed was warranted, because the head of the division had a very low opinion
of this particular individual. Disturbed by what I viewed as
the unfair, capricious nature of the request, I discussed the
matter with a trusted colleague, who advised me to act according to my conscience and give the evaluation that I believed
was merited. Recognizing that I was a young manager taking
a risk in disregarding the stated wishes of a senior executive,
I explained my rationale to my manager, put my thoughts in
writing, and then did what I felt was right and never regretted
it. I didn't hear another word about the issue and it was never
held against me—as I believe my own management ultimately
recognized that the request was highly inappropriate and it
was best just to let the whole unfortunate situation melt away.

Termination time. A talented but difficult employee of mine
had crossed a line, with cantankerous behavior that was no
longer merely just frustrating but hostile and disruptive to
productivity. While my initial probably too-tolerant Type B
reaction was to warn the employee, I consulted with a trusted
Human Resources colleague and she convinced me there was
more than enough evidence to fire the individual. She just
wanted to be sure that all prior incidents with this employee
had been documented clearly so there would be minimal
chance of future liability to the company—always prudent
advice in such matters. It turned out her guidance was excellent. The documentation was sound, the termination swift
and efficient, and that was the end of the matter. There were
no future legal repercussions, and other employees in the
department were visibly pleased to see that an employee whom

they viewed as a malcontent and negative influence had received what was deserved.

"He said / she said." While away on a company business trip, two highly regarded employees, one of whom reported to me, got into a serious dispute, each accusing the other of unprofessional behavior. The more I listened to the back-and-forth accusations, the more I had absolutely no idea whom to believe (an unfortunately common predicament in delicate employee matters!). I consulted with the manager of the employee who didn't report to me—whose experience and good judgment I greatly respected. Led mostly by her calm, thoughtful, resolutely Type B instincts, we were able to somewhat, if never completely, untangle the situation, warn both employees about the kind of conduct always expected when representing the company on business, and ultimately put the whole unpleasant incident behind us. I always felt that the other manager's unflappable Type B demeanor played the crucial role in de-escalating a potentially explosive incident and leading us to a positive outcome.

Management Insight

Management abounds with complex, delicate problems for which there may not be clear right or wrong answers. Open-communicating Type B managers are well suited to reach out and get an additional perspective (or two) from trusted colleagues—a valuable sounding board to help clarify thinking on an issue.

CHAPTER 24

Take Care of Your People and They'll Take Care of You

He was a much-decorated Vietnam veteran, a retired colonel who following his military career worked for two more decades as an executive in business. At our last management team meeting his farewell message was simple: "As we used to say in the army, 'Take care of your people and they'll take care of you.'"

I'm generally not a big fan of battlefield metaphors in business (cross fire, minefields, leading the troops into battle, and so on), as my feeling is they do a disservice to those who literally *are* risking their lives on a daily basis. But the more I've thought about my former colleague's words, the more I've come to believe they convey a fundamental management truth.

When I think back to my own years in management, my best and most productive employees invariably felt well cared for—respected, rewarded, and secure. Conversely, when employees felt, for whatever reasons, that I didn't sufficiently "have their back," loyalty quickly waned. The attitude of one of my star managers, for example, changed quickly when he felt I wasn't doing enough to forcefully advocate for his department during a period of organizational transition. In retrospect I came to believe he was right—he was an extremely valuable employee who for reasons that were more personal than rational had fallen into political disfavor. The mistake was mine and I paid a price in lost loyalty.

Similarly, when I think back on myself as an employee—as most managers of course are employees too—I worked with the greatest energy and diligence when I felt a manager had my best interests at heart and genuinely wanted to develop and advance me. But when I sensed a manager was less interested in my career and more focused on his or her advancement or survival or other purely personal objectives, there's no question it affected my productivity. I was still conscientious and professional, so the effects were subtle, almost imperceptible. The way I view it from my vantage point today is that in such circumstances I'd give 99 percent. But when I felt truly supported and valued, I'd give 110 percent.

Fortunately, many Type B individuals have, as we've seen, a natural inclination to reach out and connect with others, and this impulse can serve them well in management. Of course business is business, and management will at times require painful life-altering decisions. But even in these toughest times—think layoffs—if your employees believe you genuinely care about their well-being, you'll have the best chance of eliciting their best performance.

On the other hand, if you're more concerned with building your empire than with those who are helping you build it, safe to say it *will* be noticed. Self-interest being a powerful motivator, employees are understandably focused on their own careers. After all, as the saying goes, it's the radio station WIFM (What's in It For Me) that everyone's tuned to, all day every day.

Management Insight

Employees are most productive when they feel safe in their roles, not uncertain about their future. Type B managers often can create a working environment characterized by security more than anxiety.

PART III

Putting It Together

Throughout these chapters, we've examined the differences between Type A and Type B personalities, and the ways in which they influence management performance. While we've generally discussed Type A and Type B personalities as separate, distinct entities—and you may well know plenty of managers who conform closely to each type—it's also true that many individuals combine elements of both types. In this section we'll describe how managers can become more effective by blending these characteristics: how some Type A's can enhance their skills by adopting more relaxed Type B traits, and how some Type B's can benefit by adding elements of the more assertive Type A skill set. We'll also apply the Type A and B framework to the hiring environment, showing how Type A and B insights can help you choose the best managers—by finding individuals who are temperamentally well suited to succeed in a management role.

CHAPTER 25

For Type A Managers

Boosting the B
(Turning Down the Volume)

Are there times you feel that some of your personality traits are impeding your ability to manage as effectively as you could? Do you feel you're a Type A, possessing many of the constellation of qualities discussed in Chapter 2—the competitiveness, the aggressiveness, the urgent focus on time? Do you ever feel that the force of your personality is something of a double-edged managerial sword? You have strong leadership skills but at the same time the intensity of your authority alienates some of those around you, which results in more employee morale problems, turnover, and disengagement than you'd ideally like?

If the answer to these questions is yes, this section will be helpful to you. In Part II we examined, among other things, numerous management functions—including employee development, delegation, communication, evaluation, accountability, and so on—that have a direct effect on employee engagement, motivation, and ultimately productivity. In this section we'll examine realistic, practical ways managers can adjust their behavior and personal styles to improve management performance.

The good news is that this is entirely possible. Substantive behavioral changes are well within reach, given an individual's desire to make them. Even Drs. Friedman and Rosenman back in 1974, in *Type A Behavior and Your Heart*, stated clearly: "A number of physicians have gloomily generalized to us that 'once a Type A person, always a Type A person.' But this need not be so, as these doctors would easily discover if they studied the waning intensity of Type A behavior in certain of their own patients." In short, Type A individuals can indeed make changes in their management approach if they're sufficiently motivated to do so. Just as can Type B individuals, as we'll explore in the next chapter.

But first let's continue with our Type A analysis, examining various business situations and responses. Following are some scenarios that were introduced earlier. We'll now revisit them in greater depth, reviewing management problems that commonly occur and the behavioral changes that can help Type A's avoid them.

Ignoring minor things that seem insignificant to you, but matter to others. We saw in Chapter 11 ("Small Things Make a Big Difference"), for example, that Marcia was deeply bothered by the fact that her manager worked at such a frantic pace that he never took the time to look directly at her when they talked, but worked continually at his computer, relentlessly multitasking. We also saw in this same chapter how another team grew increasingly frustrated by being regularly kept waiting at staff meetings and how that bred disrespect.

In both of these instances the managers would have been surprised to learn that their actions had the negative effect they did. They had no idea their direct reports were perceiving their behaviors in a certain way, and would have been even more surprised to hear that these seemingly trivial events played a significant role in shaping the way they were regarded by others. Even more important from a career standpoint, they would have been shocked to learn the extent to which these behaviors could undermine their management success.

Inadvertent demoralization. We saw in Chapter 3, on motivating and demotivating, that one simple ill-chosen comment—"That's pathetic!"—from an intensely focused Type A business owner to a valued employee, who simply hadn't taken the time to look at the company's new website, had the power to disturb the employee enough to make her question whether that job was the right one for her. Never mind that the phrase "that's pathetic" wasn't even what the manager meant to communicate. She didn't at all think her employee was "pathetic." She actually felt strongly that Donna was highly capable and valuable. But just the tone and force of a simple offhand comment had unfortunate power to disturb and disrupt.

I observed this same dynamic in action many times in many different ways during my years in management. Often it wasn't what was said so much as *how* it was said. Too much high-volume excitability directed to the wrong employee is easily taken the wrong way. The fact is, many especially forceful Type A managers have the power to demoralize unintentionally, even when doing so is the furthest thing from their mind.

Out-of-control communication. Sometimes Type A management communication issues are unintentional and subtle, and sometimes they're simply—call it what it is—out of control. We saw in Chapter 5 ("Bring Me My Shoes") Cathy's manager literally shouting over the phone for a new pair of shoes to be located and brought to her for an early morning meeting. (Truth can be stranger than fiction.) This was an abuse of positional power that over time, and not too much time, resulted, predictably enough, in costly time-consuming turnover. While this incident was a bit out of the ordinary, anyone who has worked in a business setting for a good amount of time likely has his or her own collection of crazy management stories. Unchecked power can intoxicate, and intoxicated management behavior can turn toxic and unpredictable.

What's most unfortunate is that all of these situations I've just described were *entirely preventable*. They had nothing whatsoever to do with these managers' intelligence or business acumen or strategic thinking or knowledge of a specific function. Indeed, all the managers we've discussed here were smart, hardworking, and in many ways highly capable businesspeople. But they were needlessly sabotaged by actions that were within their own power to control.

So what can you as a Type A manager do to avoid such self-inflicted problems? How can you avoid being undermined by events you're barely aware of? How can you become the most effective manager possible?

It all starts with awareness and a desire to change—recognition that some level of adjustment of your management style could be beneficial. Perhaps you've seen too much turnover on your watch,

too high a level of employee disengagement, too low a level of productivity, or simply chronic interpersonal conflicts—"corporate
battles" that are sapping your emotional energy and wearing you
down. If you feel that the kind of issues described here—the small
things you're barely aware of that seem to matter more to others than
to you, the unintended consequences of the natural force of your
personality—can cause difficulties for you, a desire to change could
make good business (and even personal) sense.

How do you go about it? A constructive first step is gathering
honest feedback, gaining a consciousness of how you're perceived by
others increasing what I'd call self-awareness of your managerial
style. In short, how you come across to the rest of the world in the
normal course of business events. More specifically, the impact you
have on those in your management orbit. And most important of
all, an accurate assessment of how you interact with your direct
reports—your employees—on a daily basis. This is the thread from
which the management cloth is made.

So how exactly are you being perceived? And how do you get this
information? As with most everything in business, good decisions
start with good data.

The data can be formal (your organization may well offer 360-
degree evaluations, for example) or informal (face-to-face conversations). It's possible your HR organization may even have management
development coaches, or contractual consultants, who can help you
with this process.

Personally I always like face-to-face communication—you tend
to learn more and have the opportunity to go wherever a conversation
leads you. And who should you ask for such feedback? You can get
it from any number of trusted sources. It could be your own manager, or a mentor, or colleagues, or your Human Resources contacts,

or all of the above—people whose intuition and judgment you respect and most importantly whom you can count on to give you honest answers. Best of all are your employees—who see you most closely in your day-to-day management role. While there may be natural initial reluctance for them to be candid (you're their boss after all), if you let them know exactly what you're doing and why you're doing it, there's a good chance you'll get valuable insights from them. Be sure they understand you're sincere in these efforts and are making a genuine effort to identify and perhaps modify elements of your management approach, and completely assure them there will be no downside to their candor. This "no downside" assurance is crucial. Let them know how much you appreciate their time and honesty, and there's a reasonable possibility you'll get insights from them that no one else is in a position to give you.

In one of the examples noted earlier, had Marcia's manager ever solicited this sort of feedback, he would have found she was a straight-talking person who would have said, "You know, I have a great deal of respect for you as a businessperson. I know you're smart and dedicated. But one thing I have to tell you . . . this habit of yours of continuing to stare at your computer screen and never actually taking the time to show me the courtesy of looking me in the eye when we're speaking—it just drives me crazy!" Certainly, this would have been an easy issue to fix.

Once you have practical, actionable feedback—whether from colleagues or more formal feedback mechanisms like 360-degree surveys—and issues have been identified that seem fair and accurate to you, suggesting changes in your personal management style you'd like to make, how do you go about implementing those changes? Let's say for purposes of this discussion that your feedback indicates you want to slow down the Type A train a bit and cultivate some of those calmer, more reflective Type B ways of relating to others—more carefully attuned to the human environment around you. You don't want to make these changes because they're somehow "nice" or "sensitive" or politically correct. You want to make these changes for one reason: They can help you be more effective as a manager.

Behavioral change is never accomplished simply, like flipping a light switch. But structure and process can help you make changes and stick to them over time.

Again, it starts with the willingness and motivation to change, now aided by the data you've gathered about your own management self. Let's assume your informal research from your employees and trusted colleagues has enabled you to isolate four specific aspects of Type A behavior you'd like to change.

You'd like to react to stressful workplace situations with a more measured approach. You may have a natural tendency—many in management do—to respond quickly, strongly, and impulsively to stressful situations—"shoot first and ask questions later." But you've also noticed that this high-voltage pattern, this excitability, puts people on edge and often doesn't result in a resolution that is satisfactory—it doesn't get you the results you hoped for.

You'd like to feel—and show—less anger in interactions with one of your employees. Perhaps you're in a pattern where one of your employees, whom you see regularly and who is genuinely talented, "gets under your skin" and easily irritates you. You'd like to moderate this reaction, which does little but create an atmosphere of tension when you're working with this employee, which is often. The tension then feeds on itself; the employee senses your animosity and pushes back, and you find yourself in a dysfunctional spiral where you're now consciously avoiding contact with this person, which of course is no way to manage.

You'd like to be more flexible. One of the easiest but most insidious management traps to fall into is the "this is the way we've always done it here" mindset. It's a potential hazard for any manager who's been in the role for a while and is part of a well-entrenched culture. As a Type A individual, you're probably accustomed to exerting considerable authority and "having things your way." You might not even be fully aware of the extent that this subtly discourages honest dialogue and innovation on the part of your employees. But perhaps a part of you does realize that control, while of course necessary, can be taken to extremes—and that more flexibility in your management style could lead to better outcomes.

You don't want to slip back into old habits of non-introspection, but want to continue to be fully aware of how others perceive you. Looking ahead, you don't want to return to your old, familiar management ways. You want to maintain the hard-earned gains you've made. You like the relative calmness of your new management style—and the positive effect it seems to have on others—and you want to be sure not to backslide in the future.

How do you achieve these behavioral goals? How do you make them permanent? Following are suggestions to help you achieve your goals and consolidate the gains you've made:

Focus on one particular area at a time. Attack one behavior at a time. If you try to fight on many fronts simultaneously, you'll likely win on none of them. As a manager, you're probably multitasking more than enough already. For this type of disciplined self-improvement work, concentrate on one area to improve (for example, becoming calmer when dealing with your especially challenging employee) until you've made and maintained over time the gains you wanted to.

Isolate and document when you've successfully demonstrated the desired behavior. After an instance where you accomplished what you hoped to, take a step back and think about what you did. For instance, let's say in a meeting on a contentious topic with your talented but difficult employee you did everything you set out to do: You went in with your emotions firmly in check, you held your anger and maintained the moral high ground, and you reached an amicable resolution on a challenging issue. Write down, for yourself, for your own future reference, exactly what occurred—what worked and why it did. How an infusion of Type B equanimity and lower stress levels helped to defuse the normal tensions of your interaction and ultimately led to a more satisfactory outcome. How your more emotionally flexible approach was well received by your employee and kept a potentially combustible encounter on a productive path.

Reward and reflect (on why you were successful). Reinforce the successful repetition of the desired behavior by rewarding yourself with something you might not normally take the time to enjoy. (Not being you, of course, I have no idea what that is. It could be a bottle of champagne, a fine dinner with a friend or spouse, a box seat at a baseball game, a night at the opera, a day at the races, a special bound copy of *War and Peace*, or a wolverine hunt for all I know.) The point is, though behavioral change isn't simple, it's definitely possible—and good for you for getting it right and getting where you want to go. Play back in the theater of your mind what worked in this recent encounter—how you kept your cool in heated circumstances when perhaps, as our friend Rudyard Kipling wrote in his poem "If," *all about you are losing theirs.*

Check in periodically with your trusted management support system. Don't just rely on your own personal report card, your own perceptions of your performance, but from time to time check in with your management, your mentors, your colleagues, your trusted psychological Sacajaweas who are helping to guide you through this previously unexplored management terrain. Get their candid perceptions to make sure you're all on the same page and they're in agreement that the changes you're seeing in yourself are equally visible to others as well. Do they feel you're being more flexible in handling tense management situations? Have they seen evidence of it? Is it as clear to others as it feels to you?

Knowledge is power, and actionable insights that can help your career are extremely useful knowledge. Who wants to have their

"Letting Go"

You sometimes learn more about management from your own employees than from books or courses. I well remember a sports marketing executive who reported to me becoming frustrated by what she felt was my persistent over-involvement in the logistical details of event planning for a major tennis tournament our company sponsored. The marketing executive was professional and meticulous, with decades of experience. She was more than capable of determining menus, ticket distribution, entertainment options, and other on-site aspects of our company's sponsorship. One day when she'd had enough of my meddling, I mean management, she took me aside and said, "You know, when you're managing creative people, you'll get the best results if you just tell them what to do, not how to do it. Just give good strategic direction and then let them figure out the best way to solve the problem."

She was right of course, and from that day forward I used her guidance when managing creative individuals. But my real point here is less about creative management than about letting go—knowing when firm control is needed and when you'll get better results by backing off. So what are specific areas where Type A's will want to be vigilant about letting go?

Delegation is an obvious potential pain point. Since management is all about accomplishing work through others, you won't get much done by holding on to too much yourself. Projects will bottleneck and be delayed. Your people, and likely your own management as well, will grow frustrated. I was always impressed that as brilliant a businessperson as Warren Buffett, our "Delegator in Chief," was famed for his insistence on handing things off and giving his people extremely wide latitude. Of course, part of his brilliance doubtless involved the decisions he made about whom he initially chose to hire.

Micromanagement is the reverse side of the delegation coin. Close management where it's genuinely needed is one thing, but nettlesome micromanagement is another. Nobody likes to be micromanaged. It demoralizes, and discourages initiative. As a manager, you need to know your people and how long a leash to give them. Type A's—and indeed all managers at times, as I personally discovered—need to guard against the tendency to overmanage. My sports marketing colleague certainly didn't need me weighing in on the relative merits of Shrimp Scampi versus Chicken Cordon Bleu.

career—the source of their livelihood—undermined by actions they're unaware of? Nobody.

Substantive behavioral change is never accomplished in the blink of an eye. It's tough, disciplined work. It naturally takes time to modify patterns of responses that have been ingrained for years. But it can be done. As Drs. Friedman and Rosenman noted, they clearly observed the "waning intensity" of Type A behavior in many of their Type A patients who had a sincere desire to change.

So too in the world of management. Change is always possible as long as it genuinely starts from within. Nor should it be viewed as the correction of some kind of personal failure. Because as we've seen with numerous aspects of the Type A personality—the natural sense of authority, the urgency, the ability to execute difficult projects in tight time frames—many classic Type A attributes are vital for management success. This kind of change—"boosting the B in you and moderating the A"—should be seen less as a response to criticism than as a pathway to improvement.

A pathway to becoming the most successful manager you can.

Management Insight

Substantive behavioral change is indeed possible and, with a focused approach, can be achieved. You're not trying to change your whole personality (nor would you want to or be able to), but just to moderate certain elements you've identified—to increase your effectiveness as a manager.

CHAPTER 26

For Type B Managers

Adjusting the A
(Turning Up the Volume)

Not surprisingly, the kinds of changes Type B managers will want to make to enhance their effectiveness have an entirely different character from the kind just discussed in the prior chapter. While some Type A managers will benefit from "turning down the volume," so to speak, to moderate their naturally high-octane style, some Type B's will benefit from "turning up the volume"—responding to situations more forcefully and clearly when their natural inclination is to take a stay-on-the-sidelines approach.

If you're a more reserved and laid-back Type B sort of manager, do you ever find yourself avoiding interactions with difficult employees because you suspect they'll be thorny and you'd just rather "not get into it"? Do you find yourself regularly avoiding conflict? Do you find yourself accepting lower-quality work and less productivity than you'd ideally like from your employees because you recognize that forcing the issue may lead to tense confrontations and disturb comfortable working relationships?

If the answer to some of these questions is yes, this chapter should be valuable to you. We'll focus on very different issues and solutions than in the prior chapter. But as in that chapter, we'll focus on practical, tactical ways you can modify your management approach to improve performance. The good news, as we saw with Type A managers, is that significant behavior changes and improvements are fully possible, if you have the will to make them. So let's analyze in more detail a variety of business scenarios and management responses.

As we've seen, Type B managers, because of their more relaxed people orientation, often have the valuable ability to motivate, to build loyal teams and close, productive employee relationships. But if these relationships grow too close (and I'm not referring to anything romantic—that's a whole other topic under the heading of "inappropriate management") and there's insufficient managerial distance, problems can develop. Accordingly, here are common challenges Type B managers face:

The ostrich syndrome. The most prevalent issue involves what I would call in simple but blunt language a tendency to avoid the hard stuff. A natural, understandable tendency to look the other way and put your head in the sand, ostrich-like, when it needs to be well aboveground and staring vexing problems clearly in the eye. Conflict avoidance, not dealing directly with challenging employees—these are the kind of situations where the friendly, accommodation-seeking spirit of the Type B manager is quickly tested.

On my blog at *Forbes*, one manager wrote to me poignantly about this general subject. I'd written that successful managers aren't "daunted" by conflict: "You have to be able to handle it effectively," I noted, "or others won't want to follow." To which a reader quickly responded, "I'll be printing this off and putting it where I can read it every morning—dealing well with conflict (instead of running and hiding) has been one of my biggest challenges as a relatively new manager, so thank you for reminding me that conquering that fear of conflict is worth it! Thank you for the pep talk this morning!" Those nicely articulated feelings are hardly unique. Preferring to look away in the face of undeniable difficulty is an entirely human as well as ostrich-like response. Unfortunately, it's not one you can hope to continue for long in the management business. (Which is why we'll soon be discussing solutions, not just problems.)

Making tough decisions. A related Type B challenge is an inability to make really difficult decisions—or a conscious desire to avoid them. But the reality is the job of management abounds with tough choices—staff cuts, budget cuts, employee terminations, performance issues, and on and on. That's one of the reasons management is compensated as well as it is: It's not for everyone, and it can be filled with stress and mental anguish. Which can be hard on a too-gentle Type B. It's easier to procrastinate and put off till tomorrow or next month something you know will cause others pain. But the potential to have to make excruciating decisions is implicit in every manager's job description.

Driving for productivity. As we saw with Dave's unfortunate experience back in Chapter 4 ("Management Without High Standards Isn't Management At All"), managers are routinely expected to drive for productivity—to meet tight deadlines, to maintain exceptional quality control, and to motivate their employees and teams to go above and beyond. Competitive realities require it. Well-liked Dave delivered great rapport but not great results. And when you fail to meet even aggressive goals on a consistent basis, your own management's patience will be limited. Management is a data-driven and results-oriented enterprise. Even if you're widely regarded as a terrific person—a likable individual of unassailable character— without consistently positive results it will be hard to argue you're doing the job . . . and unfortunately you may not be for long.

So assume your initial thinking is that you could benefit by making some changes to your Type B management style. As we just described in the prior chapter, a constructive first step is to get validation from others that the kinds of changes you envision for yourself could indeed be helpful and are realistic. There's no need to repeat all the information we just provided in the last chapter, but the basic tactic of gathering honest, reliable feedback, the details on how you're perceived by others—whether by formal 360-degree evaluations or by informal in-person conversations—remains a constructive approach. As with our Type A description, you'll use your own network of managers (and former managers), mentors, colleagues, Human Resources contacts—individuals whose judgment you trust. Again, you never want to load the deck with people who will just say nice things about you. That will feel pleasant but accomplish nothing. Above all, you want objectivity, candor, and usable data. Naturally you'll want feedback from your employees—no matter what your management style, they're the ones who know your day-to-day management strengths and weaknesses best of all. And of course you'll need to give them sincere assurances that there's absolutely no downside to their honesty, that you're sincere in your desire to make personal changes in your management approach, and that their input will be extremely helpful to you.

If Dave from Chapter 4 had pushed for this kind of candid feedback from his team, it's likely one of his experienced company veterans would have told him something along the lines of "You know, Dave, we all like working for you and you're a great guy, but you just can't continue to be late for major project deadlines. That's job one around this place: Deliver big projects on time. I'd like to think I'm wrong and that your management will appreciate your many abilities and thoughtfulness as much as we all do, but I'm afraid for you they won't be too patient. We just want you to succeed and continue to be our boss."

So now you've gathered your own impressions and validated them with accurate feedback from others. Let's say it seems to be in your best interests to add a little more edge and energy and authority to your Type B demeanor. Specifically, you want to work on resolving conflict more forcefully and effectively, and you want to manage a particular team you're responsible for more tightly and productively.

As we know, behavioral change isn't accomplished overnight, but with effort and persistency over time. Accordingly, here are suggestions to help bring out the dormant "A" in you:

Accept the nature of the management role. Don't fight it. Understand it. Accept it. Make the best of it. Recognize that conflict, disagreement, and disputes are all integral threads in the fabric of management, and the sooner you fully accept this reality, the sooner you'll be able to embrace the challenges it entails. You just need to borrow a little of the resilience and coat of armor from your Type A friends—which is well within your power to do. As I described back in Chapter 16 ("The Fine Art of Managing Conflict"), a trusted mentor of mine was concerned enough to take me aside early in my career and straightforwardly tell me, "I just don't know if you can handle conflict. . . . I don't know if you have the stomach for it. Because so much of management, particularly at the higher levels, involves dealing with conflict on a regular basis." Though I never relished conflict (who does?), over the years I hardened my psychic armor and shifted my mindset and expectations so I could handle it. I made a conscious emotional adjustment. I still may never have enjoyed serious conflict, but I didn't let it unduly disturb me. I accepted it as a fundamental element of the management business and dealt with it as diligently and effectively as I could. And if I with all of my imperfections and natural reticence could do that, there's one thing I'm certain of: You can too.

Recognize that your primary obligation is not to your employees but to your own management. Repeat after me: "I AM IN MANAGEMENT." This is the job you've chosen and the job that you, as long as you continue to stay in the role, to the best of your abilities, will have to do. It doesn't mean that you won't care about your employees, or want the best for them, or treat them with dignity and respect. The very best managers invariably do. But it does mean that when difficult situations arise, as they always do—budget shortfalls that are unsustainable, disappointing financial results, performance from a well-liked individual that demonstrates he or she just can't make the grade—your primary allegiance in constructively resolving such issues is to your own management, not to the employees you like and work with closely every day. This may seem an obvious point, but I can tell you from experience it's often not adhered to. Over the years I've seen many managers identify more with their employees than with their management role. That's not, however, a sustainable position. Very early in my management career I recall being in this kind of quandary. I had a tough decision to make. I felt loyalty to an employee I personally liked and who had done good work in the past but who was now having persistent problems delivering the quality of work we needed and consequently had lost the confidence of senior management. I knew in my gut that corrective action needed to be taken, but I was initially reluctant to do it because of our personal history. For guidance, I sought out a senior colleague whose judgment I respected. I could see both sides of the issue. I explained that it was a tricky situation. He listened to my story, looked at me, and said simply, "Who's signing your paycheck?"

I got the message.

Making the tough decisions. You can't avoid them. You have to make them. So summon some of that Type A backbone and make them as well as you can with as much empathy and dignity as you can. In my own experience, when hard messages were delivered to me, it meant a great deal to me to have someone sitting across the table look me in the eye and communicate in plain, thoughtful English exactly what was happening and why. Look at it this way: If you feel you're incapable of making a hard decision and then communicating bad news because you don't want to hurt your employees . . . well, if you don't do it someone else will, and they'll probably do it with less sensitivity than you, so it might as well be you. In Chapter 17 we talked about the importance of empathy when firing someone. The same dynamic holds true for any tough message. Communicating thoughtfully and with empathy: It's a valuable management skill at which many Type B's excel.

Recognize that well-conceived employee objectives are always a loyal ally in your management mission. This is one of the key reasons why we discuss management by objectives at the length we do here. Apologies for any repetition, but the point is crucial. You want to be more effective in managing for productivity? You want to increase the odds that team members collaborate well and projects are successfully delivered on deadline? Make sure the results you want to achieve are recorded clearly and unmistakably in your employees' job objectives. Then as the year progresses it's not just you being a tougher manager than you're really comfortable being—it's you rationally managing to goals you've all agreed to. And if the goals are aggressive—"ambitious but attainable" is good language—it's not you being unreasonably demanding . . . it's simply you managing productively to standards that have been mutually and thoughtfully established. It makes no sense at all to spend substantial time carefully developing employee objectives if you're not going to use them. They'll be a vital ally to you in tightening up your management style.

As we discussed in the last chapter for Type A managers, a desire to change certain aspects of your management style is in no way an admission of personal failure. We know Type B managers typically have many innately outstanding qualities—their natural calmness, their open communication style, the rapport they build with their employees—that aren't easy to find but are vital to management success. But no manager wants to be perceived as weak. So when constructive change is needed, it's entirely possible that adjusting your style by "turning up the volume" and adding a dash more authority to your repertoire will only enhance your effectiveness.

As with so much in life, a balanced approach often yields excellent results.

Management Insight

No one in management ever wants to be thought of as "weak." There's never a good excuse to abuse authority, but there *are* times when tightening control will help Type B's achieve A+ results.

CHAPTER 27

The Balance Benefit

An underlying theme of this book is the virtue of balance—the managerial benefits of centered equilibrium. Too much frenetic Type A oversight or too much passive Type B supervision rarely leads to optimal outcomes.

What exactly do I mean by "balance" as it applies to the practice of management?

At an operational level, a core management skill is the ability to deal effectively with multiple priorities. If as a manager you have a reasonably large span of control, you doubtless have many projects, people, and budget dollars, not to mention intransigent unresolved issues, in your purview. Tilt too far in any one direction and the managerial ship sails easily off course. Type B managers who know their business and are measured in their approach to it—not too intensely focused in any single direction—are well equipped to handle the multiple challenges the role presents.

At a psychological level, a balanced personality is just a solid temperament for a manager. Good management requires sound, rational decisions, assessing opportunity and risk, and making the best choices, often in stressful situations without all the facts known. If, as a Type B individual, you can build a reputation as a person who remains calm under pressure but isn't afraid to take action when you need to, that's a valuable combination that should attract the attention of those above you—and serve you well throughout your management career.

Simply put, successful management requires balance in what you do and how you do it.

You need authority, but not so much it alienates. Come on too strong, wield your authority with too heavy a hand and your employees will resent it. Come on too softly, wield your authority with too weak a hand and your employees will take advantage of it. Somewhere in the middle lies balance: a level of authority that's neither feared nor ignored, but respected. Authority that delivers results.

You need to be a juggler, capable of keeping many "balls in the air." The challenge of balancing multitasked priorities is common to all managers. One constant throughout my years in management was that I was literally *never* caught up with all that needed to be done. Unlike many individual contributors, managers are always multitasking, always dealing with multiple projects and priorities, plus of course the ever-challenging individuals who report to them. Focus too intently on any single matter and others will inevitably be neglected. Finding the right balance among priorities, the right timing to not "drop any of the balls," is a key ingredient to management success.

Requiring from your employees a quality and quantity of work that is demanding but realistic. The results you require from your employees—both the specific objectives you set and the more general expectations you hold—need to balance the demanding with the realistic. If you continually push for results that can't be achieved, you'll frustrate your employees. But if you set the bar too low, you won't be doing enough to drive performance and you'll frustrate your own management. Again, somewhere in the middle lies the right level of expectations, those that will optimize performance.

Productive relationships with those both above and below. Managers at all levels, from supervisors to the C-suite, have to balance the needs of their own management with the needs of their employees. Lean too far in either direction—satisfy your own management on the backs of the employees, or listen too closely to your employees while ignoring your own management—and you'll hit bumps in the managerial road. Pleasing different constituencies with vastly different agendas is an inherent challenge of the role.

The balance between work life and home life may be the most important equilibrium of all. Ideally you work hard enough to get the results that are required, but not so hard that burnout and fatigue set in. I worked at one time with a CEO who firmly believed you could only do your best thinking when you were relaxed and your mind was clear and uncluttered, and consequently insisted that *all* employee vacation time be taken—a welcome change to the common and regrettable current tendency to leave unused vacation time on the table.

Now about that budget . . . I don't need to say a lot about balancing this one. No matter where in business you reside—whether you manage a global division of two thousand or a modest department of two—one thing I say with certainty is that you'll find neither patience nor sympathy for an unexpectedly overspent budget. So that part of your operation had best be in balance too.

Management Insight

Equilibrium is a valuable managerial quality. Type B managers who know their operations well and stay centered and steady—not leaning too far in any one direction—are squarely on the right track.

CHAPTER 28

How to Make Good Management Hires

One of the most important decisions you'll make as a manager is who you hire as a manager.

The higher you go in an organization, of course—and the broader your own span of control—the more vital to your success your own managers become. In this chapter, we'll examine how insights about Type A and Type B personalities can help you select and hire the best managers—those who have the greatest likelihood of success.

As we've seen, choosing the right people for management is no easy task. Statistics detailed in Chapter 1 from Gallup and other research organizations show that employee engagement rates on a national basis consistently hover around the 30 percent mark—meaning approximately seven out of ten employees are not emotionally committed to their organizations—at a lost productivity cost estimated by Gallup at over $450 billion a year. Even if such macrolevel data is imprecise, the main point is unmistakable: There's an army of disengaged employees out there and an army of managers not doing a satisfactory job in fully engaging them.

At a more micro level, I recall a conversation I once had with a Human Resources executive with whom I worked closely. We were discussing the constellation of qualities needed for management success when she sighed and said simply, "Good managers are hard to find." Six simple words I suspect many in Human Resources organizations will agree with.

Given this backdrop of inherent challenge, how can you help your company avoid hiring the wrong kind of people and guide it toward hiring those who will succeed in the management role? Is there any way to predict managerial success?

Full disclosure at the outset: Human nature never being 100 percent predictable, there are no surefire models to predict managerial success. That having been said, there *are* essential qualities successful managers can't do without and, conversely, red flags that should go up immediately in certain circumstances as a managerial warning. Think of the Type A and Type B behavioral qualities as a spectrum that starts with pure Type A qualities (ultra-competitive, highly aggressive, and controlling) on the far left, and pure Type B qualities (laid-back to the point of near somnolence, minimal sense of time urgency) on the far right. Toward the middle you'll find a blending of qualities, with Type A's possessing some Type B characteristics left of center along the spectrum, and Type B's having some Type A characteristics right of center.

From a hiring perspective, any potential manager who appears to reside very far out at either end of the spectrum will likely encounter substantive problems in a management role. It's common sense: An ultra-aggressive Type A will be hard to work for and an ultra-relaxed Type B will have a hard time getting things done. As an assessor of managerial talent, you'll want to be wary of those at the spectrum's margins and look more toward those closer to the spectrum's center. As a practical matter, it's unlikely you'll be dealing with many pure Type B's, as the vast majority of them will self-select out of any management role—having little interest in the long hours, hard work, and discipline it entails. But highly motivated pure Type A's—those are candidates you may well encounter.

Let's now consider specific personal qualities integral to management success—essential qualities you just can't do without. Throughout my career I can say with certainty that every highly respected successful manager I worked with or for possessed the six qualities described here. Conversely, any glaring weakness in these areas was a significant obstacle to long-term success. (Note the phrase "highly respected" in my definition above—no doubt at times it's possible to be successful in terms of rising in a corporate hierarchy without being widely respected. Those of us who've spent significant time in the corporate world have all seen it. But in this context I'd consider that a lower standard of success, and would argue that those who were really most successful excelled in all of these areas.)

I call them the "6 C's": Conflict, Communication, Competence, Collaboration, Confidence, and Conscience.

Conflict. A good manager has to be able to handle conflict. You get it from all sides: sometimes unreasonable demands from those above you and howls of protests from those below. Being able to address such conflicting needs in a reasonable way—satisfying the general while maintaining the troops' loyalty—is critical. While you don't have to love conflict, you have to be at least somewhat comfortable in the fray. No conflict-avoiders need apply.

Communication. All good managers are effective communicators. Trite but true. Any relationship—be it personal or business—falters on weak communication. You can't be emotionally stingy when praise for an employee is deserved, or say nothing when corrective action is needed. Every really effective manager I knew was intuitive, perceptive—and an open, honest communicator.

Competence. Basic but by no means unimportant. Without a sufficient level of technical competence, it won't be easy for a manager to gain the respect of those he or she is managing—or to make sound decisions. Of course at higher levels managers with a wide span of control often have responsibility for areas they're not expert in, but they still need enough familiarity with the operations "to know what they don't know," so they can run the area intelligently. In short, competence is foundational. This may seem obvious, but over the years I worked with numerous managers who simply didn't have enough technical competence in the areas of which they were put in charge. Inevitably this led to problems.

Collaboration. As discussed in Chapter 7, on team building, very little of importance is ever accomplished in a sizable organization without many hands touching it. As we've seen, the best managers invariably are strong communicators and collaborators—core Type B attributes—adept at working with all kinds of people and bringing out the best in them. If a prospective manager has difficulty collaborating—if his or her history indicates a pattern of problems getting along with others—this can be a knockout factor. The only exception I'd make is if a particular manager was so brilliant or his or her technical skills were so unique that the manager would really bring game-changing benefits to an organization. I worked with only a couple of these during my career, and in such cases it was worth accepting less collaboration and the drama that ensued. But in the vast majority of cases, effective managers need to get along with people. All kinds of people. All the time.

Confidence. Management is no place for the emotionally fragile. For the reasons already mentioned—being regularly buffeted from all sides—you have to be able to take a punch (figuratively if not literally) and come back the next day—or more likely in the next ten minutes—with a positive attitude. An ample dose of self-assurance is a valuable managerial asset.

Conscience. The most respected managers I knew had a conscience. They were excellent role models. They always wanted to do the right thing—for their own management, for their employees, for their organization. Some readers might disagree and say, no, all you really need to succeed is the ability to please your own boss on the backs of your direct reports. There's some truth to this; it happens. But over the long term, managers of this stripe pay a high price in terms of employee morale, productivity, and retention. It's possible these managers will "succeed" in their own careers, but they won't win respect.

Let's turn now to one of the most common pitfalls of how managers are chosen. I call it the "Strong Performer Trap." It's the alluring Venus flytrap of management selection.

It's easiest to illustrate this point with a hypothetical example. Let's say a manager on the Bobcat Tracking Team leaves your company. To replace him, we'll assume the company prefers to promote from within, rather than hiring from outside—a worthy objective that's beneficial for employee morale if the process is handled well. It always makes good business sense to give talented, motivated people an opportunity.

But just who will your company promote, and why? All too often management decides to replace a departing manager with the most technically proficient individual contributor in the department—aka the strongest performer—regardless of how well suited that person may be for the special demands of a management role.

Let's say in this hypothetical case management decides to promote Ted. Our star performer Ted is a tireless tracker of bobcats and a meticulous creator of backcountry topographical maps detailing their habitats—he's by far the most valuable member of the company's seven-person Bobcat Tracking Team. But Ted is also a lone wolf— he's a highly motivated Type A who performs best when working in a solitary manner, keeping late nocturnal hours and pursuing a project with single-minded intensity. No question he's an outstanding technical specialist. But does he possess the people-oriented and team-oriented qualities managers need? Let's consider the "6 C's" described earlier in this chapter.

Ted is unquestionably **competent**, so that's a solid foundation to build on. And he's an individual of **conscience** with high ethical standards who is justifiably **confident** in his abilities, so those are positives too.

But is Ted a strong **communicator** and **collaborator**? As part of his emotional makeup, does he possess these classic Type B skills?

"Clear Career Paths Count"

Since so many aspects of management are uncontrollable, it's always nice to find one that has the ability to motivate large numbers of employees and is well within an organization's power to control. Specifically? I'm referring to the development of clear career paths. During my decades in management, I worked in many different Human Resources environments. These included times where career paths, and thus promotional opportunities, were consistent and available—and leaner times when for a variety of reasons (salary freezes, mergers, restructuring of job classifications, etc.) promotional opportunities were slim. As a manager, the effects I observed on employees during these varying career climates were unmistakable. At times when career paths were clear, individuals were more motivated, with tangible goals to work toward. At times when career paths were closed, individuals were less motivated, less focused, more uncertain. The prospect of career advancement is a powerful motivator.

It's only natural. Talented people want to advance. They want to get ahead. Type A's, Type B's—no matter the nuances of your personality—the desire to achieve is universal. As an old advertising slogan once succinctly put it, "Americans want to succeed, not merely survive." As do people everywhere. Which is why it makes excellent business sense for organizations of all sizes to develop and maintain thoughtfully structured career path systems—a valuable HR function. This needn't be a painfully expensive proposition. Even if at times the dollar value associated with an individual promotion may be slight, the perceived value for that employee in a particular corporate culture may still be substantial.

A work environment with the opportunity for upward mobility—as opposed to one that is stagnant—can make the difference between a workforce that is engaged and one that is adrift. From a financial standpoint, the maintenance of a solid career path system isn't a huge capital investment. But it's a sound investment when it comes to human capital.

Actually Ted prefers to work quietly and by himself, lone wolf style, diligently tracking a bobcat deep in the backcountry miles from headquarters. And he strongly dislikes the confrontations and entanglements of interpersonal **conflict**—truth be told he much prefers the company of bobcats, raccoons, and mule deer to the incessant chatter of humans.

In short, all attributes considered, Ted, the team's longtime star, isn't really a good prospect for promotion to management. Yet all too often what happens is that Ted—or excellent individual contributors like him—will be promoted into management and will founder in the new role, disliking both the nettlesome human interactions and being stuck in the office, not the field. So things don't work out. Ted has trouble managing, and his employees have trouble with him. Then what happens next? All too often the organization loses another manager and, even worse, may lose one of its most valuable individual contributors as well.

My point is not that you never want to make managers out of strong individual performers—that would be an unreasonable position of course—*but don't just automatically default to that option.* If you're a manager of managers (or perhaps an HR specialist), look carefully at potential candidates' broader interpersonal skill set. Are

"The Narcissist's Edge"

Beware the allure of too much charm.

A recent study from the University of British Columbia shows that narcissists excel in job interviews—regularly presenting themselves more successfully than equally qualified but more modest candidates.[1] Narcissism, derived from the Greek myth of Narcissus, who fell in love with his reflection, involves (per the definition from *Psychology Today*) "arrogant behavior, a lack of empathy for other people, and a need for admiration"—qualities consistently exhibited at work and in relationships. Narcissists are impulsive, grandiose, and tend not to work well with others. Thus, the importance of management making sound decisions in avoiding hiring narcissists whenever possible.

This new study, however, suggests the opposite actually occurs—since the outgoing, charismatic personalities of narcissists enable them to excel in interview settings. "A job interview is one of the few social situations where narcissistic behaviors such as boasting actually create a positive impression," said Del Paulhus, psychology professor at the University of British Columbia and the study's lead author. Normally, people are bothered by such behavior—but evidently not in an interview setting. The research noted that "narcissists tended to talk about themselves, make eye contact, joke around and ask the interviewers more questions. As a result, the study found that people rated narcissists as more attractive candidates for the position."

What are the study's key lessons? Rather than being impressed by superficial likability, hiring managers should concentrate on an individual's "potential long-term fit in an organization." Which is why it's crucial for key hiring decision

> makers to focus on a candidate's actual prior results—verifiable
> hard data—rather than being swayed by charm and force of
> personality.

they good collaborators, communicators, and conflict resolvers, for
example? This can help you determine whether they really have the
right stuff to succeed in management, and not just in a bobcat-
tracking role.

Management Insight

Given the unpredictability of human behavior, there are no
100 percent certain ways to predict how someone will perform in management. But there *are* ways to improve your
odds of selection success, such as looking holistically at a
candidate's skills and personality. Strong team-oriented and
people-oriented qualities—core Type B attributes—are very
often part of a successful manager's makeup.

CHAPTER 29

Many Hats

By now it should be abundantly clear that management has more than a little complexity and that outstanding managers are both valuable and elusive. When I first heard this notion about the scarcity of good managers, I thought it strange. All companies are loaded with managers—surely there must be scads of outstanding ones around! But if you deconstruct the qualities of effective management, you find an odd combination of skill sets from a wide variety of different professions that are all parts of the management whole.

Let's consider the many hats worn. First, of course, you need reasonable technical knowledge of your own business if you hope to have "street cred" with those you're managing. But such basic competence is really just "table stakes," so let's assume technical proficiency is in place. Whether you're a Type A or Type B—raring to go or slower to react—there are still (at least) five more professional skill sets that will serve you well:

You have to be a psychologist. Good managers understand their employees—what motivates them and what demoralizes them. Good managers are intuitive. You have to be able to relate to your direct reports in a way that makes them *want* to do their best.

You need the inspirational abilities of a coach. With big projects on the line and deadlines looming, there will be many times when you'll need to exhort, inspire, and encourage your directs to do their best. Coaching—constructively guiding your employees toward desired goals—is a key piece of the managerial mix. Taking the time to understand your employees and coaching them effectively are both areas where Type B managers do well.

It also helps to have the authority of a law enforcement officer. (OK, so this role isn't quite as natural for a Type B.) At times, such as when the proverbial Really Big Project is careening off the track, being a nice, warm, encouraging coach just won't get the job done. At these highly stressful moments when immediate corrective action is required, you need authority and lots of it.

You need the meticulousness of an accountant. Chances are as a manager you'll have budgetary responsibility. The implicit assumption is that you'll have a reasonably high degree of financial acumen, and you'll get no sympathy or patience from your own management if you don't. In several organizations I worked in, going mistakenly over budget was equivalent to purchasing a one-way ticket to a Siberian labor camp. As one senior executive I knew always implored her staff: "Above all, *know your numbers*." Her counsel was simple, direct, and made complete business sense.

It pays to have the tact of a diplomat. All managers have multiple constituencies: employees, your own management, boards, customers, sales forces, etc. You have to be able to relate well to those above, below, and all around you: Different groups will have different agendas. Pay too much attention to any single constituency—please one group too much at the expense of another—and it's a safe bet problems will ensue.

Many people are first promoted into management for their strong technical skills—the table stakes noted at the outset—and solid knowledge of their own business. But that's only a fraction of the managerial equation. All managers wear many hats. Everyone has his or her strengths and weaknesses, but if you're completely lacking any of these related professional skill sets, management may well prove a challenging endeavor.

····················· **Management Insight** ·····················

A unique challenge of management is the unusual combination of professional skill sets the role requires. A Type B manager's flexibility is an asset when wearing many hats.

CHAPTER 30

Your Own Skin

In the end, it's hard enough being yourself in life and even harder to try to be someone else. While it can make good personal and business sense to tinker at the behavioral margins—to turn down your personal volume, to turn up your volume, to add some B, to adjust the A—ultimately you have to develop a managerial style that works for you. A style that feels right, feels natural, fits comfortably with the person you are.

As we've seen throughout these pages, management is nothing if not a many-faceted discipline. There are many skills to learn, many hats to wear. It took years, for instance, for Phil Jackson to learn that it could be effective to coach basketball players—*professional basketball players*, of all people, who would have thought!—with his own odd blend of Zen and Lakota Sioux philosophy. And for Warren Buffett to become comfortable enough in his own commonsense and considerable financial acumen to give the people who surrounded him the space they needed to make the best decisions. Neither of these accomplished managers was born with these managerial abilities; they developed and evolved them over time. Like all outstanding managers, they found unique styles that suited their unique personalities. Most of all they were comfortable with who they were, comfortable enough to be creative while still being true to their own instincts.

I knew early on, given the basic components of my personality, that I'd never be successful in management trying to be a highly authoritative, command and control kind of boss. It wasn't me and never would be. But I found over time that I could combine a quieter, lower-key Type B approach with a healthy respect for goals, deadlines, and an insistence on receiving high-quality work in a timely manner. Did I make mistakes along the way? Only a few thousand, as I've noted before. But did I ultimately find a management style, a suit of clothes that suited my personality . . . and was I able to do some good work for my company? In the long run I believe I did.

It all comes down to being comfortable in your own management skin. Don't for a nanosecond assume that because you're a Type B kind of person—more reserved, laid-back, even introverted—management is a game you can't play. What matters is how you choose to play it.

Once you gain that confidence in your own abilities—the confidence that enables you to take the difficult actions you need to but to do so in a way that's neither demeaning nor ineffectual and is true to your own managerial DNA—you'll have the basic tools you'll need to move forward.

My hope is these tools will serve you well for many years—in an important, demanding, and rewarding profession.

APPENDIX

General Douglas MacArthur's Principles of Leadership

When I first became a manager in 1988, I knew nothing about management, so I read everything about the subject I could find. Many of the books were long and didn't feel as practical as I needed, but there was one message that made a lasting impression. It was a one-page appendix at the back of a textbook I no longer recall. The page was titled "General Douglas MacArthur's Principles of Leadership." They consisted of seventeen brief bullet points.

While the language of his leadership principles was perhaps a little old-fashioned and military-flavored and reflected the gender orientation of the time, there was something in their simplicity and moral clarity that felt right to me. They were more useful from a people-management standpoint than anything else I could find. So I made a copy of that page and kept it in my desk drawer, referring to it often in those early days for guidance and direction.

Over the next quarter century I changed office locations many times, and as I gradually grew more comfortable in the role of management, I didn't refer to the page as often and at some point misplaced it and forgot about it.

As I was getting ready to retire from the corporate world in 2012, I was cleaning out old files when I came across that misplaced, much-handled, now yellowed piece of paper. Rereading it, I felt it was as meaningful as I'd remembered, as fundamentally valuable for managers at Google or Facebook or Alibaba, say, as for officers at West Point. The principles are:

- Do I heckle my subordinates or strengthen and encourage them?
- Do I use moral courage in getting rid of subordinates who have proven themselves beyond doubt to be unfit?
- Have I done all in my power by encouragement, incentive, and spur to salvage the weak and erring?
- Do I know by NAME and CHARACTER a maximum number of subordinates for whom I am responsible? Do I know them intimately?
- Am I thoroughly familiar with the technique, necessities, objectives, and administration of my job?
- Do I lose my temper at individuals?
- Do I act in such a way as to make my subordinates WANT to follow me?
- Do I delegate tasks that should be mine?
- Do I arrogate everything to myself and delegate nothing?
- Do I develop my subordinates by placing on each one as much responsibility as he can stand?
- Am I interested in the personal welfare of each of my subordinates, as if he were a member of my family?
- Have I the calmness of voice and manner to inspire confidence, or am I inclined to irascibility and excitability?
- Am I a constant example to my subordinates in character, dress, deportment, and courtesy?

- Am I inclined to be nice to my superiors and mean to my subordinates?
- Is my door open to my subordinates?
- Do I think more of POSITION than JOB?
- Do I correct a subordinate in the presence of others?

A biographer of General MacArthur, William Addleman Ganoe, working with General Jacob Devers, developed this list. It reflected the leadership qualities they observed in MacArthur over decades. Ganoe believed the principles had universal value. "I found all those who had no trouble from their charges," he wrote, "from General Sun Tzu in China to George Eastman of Kodak fame, followed the same pattern almost to the letter."

From Type A Behavior and Your Heart
By Meyer Friedman, MD, and Ray H. Rosenman, MD

While this passage, written in 1974, was not specifically directed at the management environment, it could well have been. As the title states, individuals can indeed change Type A behavior, if there is a desire to do so.

You Can Change Your Behavior Pattern

A number of physicians have gloomily generalized to us that "once a Type A person, always a Type A person." But this need not be so, as these doctors would easily discover if they studied the waning intensity of Type A behavior in certain of their own patients after they had survived a very severe myocardial infarction. These survivors may shed many of their Type A traits. For example, they no longer appear to be harried by their former sense of time urgency. They no longer hurry the speech of others, nor flagellate themselves attempting to think about or to perform two or more things simultaneously; no longer do they fret if they must wait in line for service, or for a delayed plane departure, or for an automobile, in front of their own, that may be moving too slowly for their taste; and no longer do they estimate life and its enjoyment in terms of acquired "numbers."

Having ventured so very close to the "other country" where there is neither time nor numbers, these survivors demonstrate an awareness of the only truly important "number" in their life, namely, the one indicating the number of days that have been allotted to them to remain on this planet.

How High-Performing Companies
Motivate Their People

One of the best and simplest ways to validate sound management practices is to study closely what high-performing companies do. Toward this end, a recent study by Towers Watson, a global benefits consulting firm, showed that following basic principles of sound management—treating employees well, offering attractive long-term career opportunities, providing highly respected leadership—indeed paid off in strong performance.

The study, "Tracking People Priorities and Trends in High-Performance Companies," examined trends in employee opinions over a five-year period. The research identified a high-performing group of companies, which cut across industry sectors, comprised of twenty-six organizations that outperformed peers in "financial performance" and "employee opinion scores." The study showed that four specific areas above all others contributed to these organizations' success:

Career development. Nothing kills the motivation of talented individuals like lack of career development opportunities. Employees in these high-performing companies were satisfied with the "emphasis on valuing and fostering talent, and the availability of long-term career opportunities and training." Note the emphasis on *long term*. In a business environment where long-term loyalty and opportunities are often in increasingly short supply, it's no surprise this quality resonates.

Empowerment. High-performing organizations excel in providing "open, supportive cultures that encourage new ideas and empower staff." They received high scores on measures such as "Most of the time it is safe to speak up in this company." Indeed, tolerance of respectfully and professionally expressed differences of opinion is a key element of a healthy corporate culture.

Rewards and recognition. Employees at these high performers were "increasingly satisfied" with compensation, benefits, and non-monetary recognition. The organizations were seen as generally showing appreciation for contributions when appropriate. Not at all surprisingly, a sentiment that scored well in these organizations was the phrase "My supervisor values my contributions."

Leadership. Employees in this high-performing group were satisfied with senior leaders' ability to "communicate down the line" to everyone, as well as to make decisions "consistent with company values." It was seen as critical for leaders to "walk the talk, not talk the walk." As we've discussed at length earlier, leaders will always benefit from leading by example.

There's nothing shocking about these results. Regardless of whether one is a Type A or Type B manager, you'll never go wrong by focusing on developing your employees, building a constructive culture, rewarding those who deserve it, and behaving in a manner that earns admiration.

But just because something is common sense doesn't mean it's commonly practiced. This study demonstrates that a highly motivated workforce is a valuable financial asset. It's a data-driven reminder that fundamentally sound management practices never go out of style. Because they work.

NOTES

Chapter 1

1. The three studies noted here are: "State of the American Workplace: Employee Engagement Thoughts for U.S. Business Leaders," by Gallup, 2013; "2012 Global Workforce Study—Driving Strong Performance in a Volatile Global Environment," by Towers Watson, 2012; "Engaging Employees: What Drives Employee Engagement and Why It Matters," by Dale Carnegie Training, 2012.

2. Letter "From the CEO," Jim Clifton, Gallup Chairman and CEO. "State of the American Workplace: Employee Engagement Thoughts for U.S. Business Leaders," by Gallup, 2013.

Chapter 2

1. *Type A Behavior and Your Heart*, by Meyer Friedman, MD, and Ray Rosenman, MD, Fawcett Publications, 1974.

Chapter 10

1. *The One Minute Manager*, Kenneth Blanchard and Spencer Johnson, William Morrow and Company, 1982.

Chapter 11

1. "Ad Age Advertising Century: The Top 100 Campaigns," *Ad Age*, March 29, 1999.

Chapter 13

1. "Why Top Young Managers Are in a Nonstop Job Hunt," by Monika Hamori, Jie Cao, and Burak Koyuncu, *Harvard Business Review*, July 2012.

Chapter 14

1. "Study on Employee Engagement Finds 70% of Workers Don't Need Monetary Rewards to Feel Motivated," by Make Their Day and Badgeville, June 2013.

Chapter 15

1. To learn more about ADD/ADHD, you can visit the websites of the American Deficit Disorder Association (add.org) and Dr. Russell Barkley (russellbarkley.org), an ADD/ADHD specialist who assisted me for my original Forbes.com article on the topic—and there are numerous other excellent resources as well.

Chapter 17

1. Study details: "One Out of Every Two Managers Is Terrible at Accountability," by Darren Overfield and Rob Kaiser, *Harvard Business Review*, November 8, 2012; "2013–2014 Talent Management and Rewards Study—North America," Towers Watson, December 2013.

Chapter 19

1. *Tap Dancing to Work: Warren Buffett on Practically Everything, 1966–2012*, A *Fortune* magazine book, by Carol J. Loomis, Portfolio/Penguin, 2012.
2. "7 Vital Trends Disrupting Today's Workplace," research by TINYpulse, December 2013.

Chapter 22

1. *Leading with Intention: Every Moment Is a Choice*, by Mindy Hall, Copper Bay Press, October 2014.
2. "When It Comes to Business Leadership, Nice Guys Finish First," study conducted by Green Peak Partners and Cornell School of Industrial and Labor Relations, June 2010.

Chapter 28

1. "Self-Presentation Style in Job Interviews: The Role of Personality and Culture," by Delroy Paulhus, Bryce Westlake, Stryker Calvez, and P. D. Harms, *Journal of Applied Social Psychology*, October 2013.

ACKNOWLEDGMENTS

Many, many thanks to Janet Rosen, my excellent agent, who always seemed to have faith in me even though I'd been away from writing for a quarter century for a career in business. And to Jeanette Shaw, my meticulous editor, who gently but firmly pushed me toward something better, as all good managers do.

ABOUT THE AUTHOR

Victor Lipman was a Fortune 500 company frontline manager and executive for nearly twenty-five years. Before that, he was a journalist for a decade. He's currently president of Howling Wolf Management Training LLC and writes regularly about management for *Forbes* and *Psychology Today*.